TAE KWON DO FOR BEGINNERS

A karate program
of fitness and
self-defense

BY WERNER AND FRANZ BUSEN

WITH ROBERT HOFLER

PHOTOGRAPHS BY KLAUS LAUBMAYER

A FIRESIDE BOOK · PUBLISHED BY SIMON & SCHUSTER, INC. · NEW YORK

DESIGNED BY BARBARA MARKS

MANUFACTURED IN THE UNITED STATES OF AMERICA
1 3 5 7 9 10 8 6 4 2
LIBRARY OF CONGRESS CATALOGING IN PUBLICATION DATA

Busen, Werner.
Tae kwon do for beginners.

"A Fireside book."
1. Karate.   2. Exercise.   3. Self-defense.
I. Busen, Franz.   II. Hofler, Robert.   III. Title.
GV1114.3.B87   1987   796.8'153   86–26067

ISBN: 0-671-61138-0

We dedicate this book to our parents,
Adelheid and Franz Busen,
and to our brother, Peter,
for always believing in and supporting us.

WERNER AND FRANZ BUSEN

Thanks to Klaus Laubmayer, my dear friend and photographer, whose pictures enhance the text and to Michele Pietra for styling the photographs.

Thanks to Susan Bearden (Ford Model Agency) for playing a part in the photographic sequences.

To Comme des Garçons, Fernando Sanchez and Devereaux, for supplying our wardrobe.

Special thanks to Charles Rue Woods for coming up with the idea and to Barbara Gess for her editorial guidance.

And to our agent, Asher Jason, many thanks for steering the ship ever so wisely.

CONTENTS

INTRODUCTION

We came to tae kwon do for purely superficial reasons: We wanted to look great. And what's wrong with that? Overweight, with muscles that were large but undefined due to weight lifting, we were looking for an exercise regimen that would give us the kind of body that you order out for: well-proportioned, defined, slim, strong, flexible, and healthy—in that order. Physical appearance is everything, we told ourselves. What you see is what you are.

Then we discovered tae kwon do. With tae kwon do, fitness is the result of both physical *and* mental conditioning. It is a means that leads you to not only a more acute state of awareness, but a consciousness radically different from what most of us in the West possess—of ourselves, our bodies, and our physical as well as mental capabilities.

WHAT IS TAE KWON DO?

Tae kwon do is the Korean style of karate. There are literally dozens of karate disciplines: Kyuokushin, kung-fu, kempo, tai-boxing, and jujitsu are a few. Tae kwon do is another. *Tae* means to jump, strike, or blow with the feet. *Kwon* translates as fist. It designates hand techniques. And *do* means "the way," in other words, the moral content and the spiritual background of this martial art.

The history of tae kwon do can be traced back almost two thousand years. In the beginning, there was a simple kind of martial art called subak, which focused on hand techniques, such as punches and blocks. At this time, the Korean peninsula contained three kingdoms: Sulla, Baekche, and Koguryo; and it was in Sulla, the weakest of the three, that subak was practiced as a kind of tournament fighting technique. Because of its growing military discipline, Sulla in time came to dominate the two other kingdoms. It was, however, a might which was not built upon sheer military power. Tempered by the teachings of a monk, Won Kwang, the soldiers of Sulla also learned the importance of mercy when fighting, and a creed of honor and respect for their rulers, their opponents, and themselves.

When the kingdom of Sulla fell in A.D. 935, to be replaced by the Koryo dynasty, a new kind of unarmed combat gained wide acceptance. Taekyon, unlike subak, focused on kicks and leg techniques. Eventually, however, the hand techniques of subak were incorporated into taekyon.

The Koryo dynasty lasted approximately five centuries, and during this time, the martial arts flourished and received royal patronage. But with the eventual demise of the dynasty, they were given less attention. Then, in 1909, when the Japanese occupied Korea, the arts were actually outlawed. Taekyon was performed only in secret. After World War II, General Choi Hong Hi revived the old taekyon and subak techniques, and in 1955 he, along with a select group of historians and teachers, established tae kwon do as the national martial arts of Korea.

Today General Choi Hong Hi is president of the International Tae Kwon Do Federation. In the United States tae kwon do has grown to such an extent that there are many federations to promote and govern the thousands of tournaments and schools which practice its discipline. The United States Tae kwon Do Federation and the Tae Kwon Do Instructors Association are only two of many such organizations. Today, even celebrities practice tae kwon do as a way to achieve fitness and health, and so the number of students has grown, from 4 million in 1975 to over 10 million today.

As America continues to be more fitness conscious, however, it is sometimes very easy to overlook the spiritual aspect of tae kwon do. As the monk Won Kwang taught the soldiers of Sulla, sparring must be tempered by respect and mercy for your opponents and yourself. Very simply put, it is this aspect of the martial arts that is the "do" of tae kwon do. The spiritual side of tae kwon do is a difficult concept to grasp. It cannot be contained in a few concise sentences. Rather, it is something you must experience for yourself. With the hope that our experiences can be helpful to you, we relate here how we came to tae kwon do, and how its unique discipline has changed our lives physically as well as mentally.

Werner Busen:

When I started studying martial arts with tae kwon do instructors, I wasn't at all interested in "do"—or anything else that seemed foreign or philosophical. In the beginning, I wanted an effective physical fitness program with the added benefit of self-defense. Tae kwon do certainly didn't disappoint me on either of those counts. I got the body I wanted and learned how to protect myself in the dojo (classroom) and out on the street.

What I had not expected was the way in which karate would affect my self-image. Obviously, there was something more to this martial arts regimen than learning a series of kicks and punches.

When I started out as a model, I was concerned whether or not my looks would be right for the market. What kind of future could I possibly have in this most unpredictable of businesses? Would I be successful enough to model full-time? There is no social security in this business. There is no college degree in modeling to put on your resume. I soon realized that neither the past nor the future was going to be much help or comfort to me.

It was tae kwon do that began to teach me to forget the past and not worry about the future. Neither exists anyway. Both are only illusions. The key is to concentrate on what you have, to focus on the present. The present is always here.

I also learned not to dwell on my physical imperfections, both as a model and a student of the martial arts. To concentrate on your faults produces only one result: worry. And that uses up lots of energy that can be channeled to more productive ends. I learned to accept my faults and get on with life, making the most of the best that I had to offer. My mental outlook was affecting my physical performance in ways that I had not thought possible. It was a surprising discovery. Sports had been practically my whole life since I began playing soccer at the age of

eight. In fact, my first career was as a professional soccer player. For five years, until the age of 23, I was a member of the number-one soccer team in Germany. Since I had achieved success early, it wasn't necessary for me to think about why I was into soccer or where I was going with the sport or how my physical prowess had come about.

Then in a championship match, I broke my left leg. It was a very bad break and I was required to spend several weeks in a hospital bed. Lying there I had nothing to do but think: Why had my club not paid the worker's compensation they owed me? How long would the leg take to heal? Why did no one from my team visit me in the hospital? Would the leg mend properly? And so on. The longer I lay in that hospital bed the more exploited I felt, not only physically but also mentally and financially. I suddenly saw the last few years of my life as nothing more than one meaningless soccer match after another. And with practically no money, or certainly less than I expected to have at this point in my career, I decided to quit soccer. Though I had played the sport for over fifteen years, I gave it all up in less than five minutes. I was finished with it forever.

Later, after the leg had healed, I began studying for a degree in physical education. Sports were still the most important aspect of my life. They were a good release, and I enjoyed the competition. Actually, I thrived on it because I was a terrific winner—and a horrible loser. I got off on being the best, and athletics were the only way I had of being just that: the best.

Unlike sports, modeling was not something I consciously set out to do. In Düsseldorf, Germany, where I was completing my studies, a photographer asked me to model for him. It was for a sportswear ad, and at the time, I considered the assignment strictly a one-shot deal. Soon, however, I was approached by other photographers. One of them told me I needed an agent, which I did, and so it occurred to me—the jock—that perhaps there was a world beyond the locker room. In 1982, I moved to Milan, where I worked on a worldwide menswear campaign for Giorgio Armani and appeared in fashion magazines like *L'Uomo Vogue*, *Vogue Hommes*, and *Mondo Uomo* among others.

But in Milan, I ran into weight problems. Blame it on the pasta or a metabolism that was slowing down, I don't know. But there on my stomach sat the extra

Werner modeling Giorgio Armani for the Italian magazine *Mondo Uomo.* **Photo courtesy of** *Mondo Uomo.*

poundage, and as a model, I couldn't afford it. Literally.

Weight lifting developed my body. But it gave me too much bulk, which wasn't what I wanted, and it did little to take off the excess pounds. Also, as a stress exercise, it actually decreased my flexibility, making my tendons grow even tighter. Mentally, the sport was far less challenging than soccer, and I missed not having an opponent to play off. After a while, the regimen of lifting weights offered me little incentive—except, of course, bigger muscles, which I already had. One workout was like any other. It lacked the competitive edge that an opponent offers you, as in soccer or tennis.

The problem with competitive sports was that, traveling all over Europe, living out of suitcases as I did, I needed an activity that I could practice in a space no larger than a small hotel room. And without a partner.

At that time, my brother Franz was practicing an unusual form of karate called tae kwon do. With tae kwon do, he had not only become slimmer, but had been able to increase his flexibility and yet maintain a high degree of muscle tone. He also spoke a great deal about some of the so-called added benefits of tae kwon do: how it had helped him to relax and, as he said, "refocus my life."

I wasn't interested in refocusing anything, much less my life. Fitness was fitness, I thought, and if martial arts could give me the physical results I wanted, then tae kwon do seemed like the perfect exercise regimen for me.

I wasn't disappointed. I lost the extra pounds, without having to change my diet. When I couldn't work out with Franz, I was able to practice my tae kwon do techniques in the smallest of hotel rooms. After practicing tae kwon do for a few months, I did not become bored with the discipline. More important, my mental outlook slowly began to change.

As a workout program, it was more than a novelty. In fact, the more I practiced, the more I wanted to increase my expertise. The better I got, the more I wanted to learn. And, in fact, that's how the martial arts differ from fitness crazes like weight lifting or jogging: There *is* something to learn. With tae kwon do, you learn a discipline. You learn a mental attitude and physical techniques that are never completely mastered or perfected. Like all forms of karate, tae kwon do uses various colors of belts to signify a student's degree of expertise. But you never arrive at a particular goal. Your goal is to continue, to better your performance, to honor the discipline you have chosen.

With tae kwon do, I felt terrific. And I soon developed an incredible physical balance that seemed to carry over into my mental well-being too. For the first time in my life, I had the feeling that I was participating in a sport for myself. I wasn't being exploited by anybody. Also, I was learning the art of self-defense, which gave me an incredible sense of security.

In May of 1983, I moved to New York City. It was a difficult decision. My modeling career in Europe was successful enough, but I looked forward to the challenge of living in the toughest city in the world. In New York there would be fewer modeling assignments, but more competition. The challenge, though, appealed to me. I use the world "challenge" because in karate the challenge is with yourself. The word "competition" belongs to another kind of philosophical outlook, a more Western one.

When you spar, you don't win. You learn. Beating another individual proves little. Tae kwon do is a "clean" self-defense, that is to say, a bloodless self-defense. You spar in order to learn how to avoid injury in a real combat situation. You learn from your opponent's strengths, from his or her knowledge. And so you gain respect for your opponent. Remember, in all the martial arts, a match begins with a bow.

In so many competition sports, athletes are taught to hate their adversaries. In locker-room warm-ups, soccer coaches would always have us growl and curse at the members of an opposing team: "Go kill 'em!" "Let's beat their brains out."

This kind of hateful competition has no place in tae kwon do or any other style of karate. As students of the martial arts, you and your opponent share a philosophy of the mind and the body, which you both honor.

Franz and I now live on different continents. We can't work out together as often as we'd like, but whenever circumstances permit, we practice karate together. In New York City I have continued my studies in a different style of karate called "U.S. kyokushin-karate" under Saiko Shihan (Master) Shigeru Oyama. Kyokushin-karate is a Japanese style of karate and means "the true meaning of the way," or "seeking the truth through the practice and the discipline of karate."

You may ask why I switched studies. Well, Shihan Oyama's school was only a few blocks from my apartment in Manhattan. Convenience was one reason. But more important, when you study karate, it is essential that you choose a good teacher.

Saiko Shihan Oyama is one of the most skillful and respected teachers in the West. Twenty-one years ago he came to the United States from Japan with the purpose of establishing the North American headquarters of the Kyokushin organization and introducing kyokushin-karate to this country. He has dedicated his life to teaching people "the true mean-

Werner and Franz practice together whenever they can.

ing of the way," and today there are 73 branches of the Kyokushin organization in the United States with over 30 thousand members. He has made kyokushin-karate so famous in America that insiders have started calling this style of sparring "U.S. Oyama Karate."

Well, who could have a better teacher than Saiko Shihan Shigeru Oyama?

Franz and I have developed our karate program from the basics of tae kwon do. However, to make the regimen more of an all-around workout/fitness program, we have also incorporated a few kyokushin techniques. Let me explain.

Tae kwon do and U.S. kyokushin are as different as a Mercedes/Benz and a BMW. The two styles of karate share the same philosophy of mind and body, but the focus of their sparring techniques is slightly different. Tae kwon do emphasizes leg over arm techniques, approximately 70 percent to 30 percent. Leg techniques are very useful for keeping an opponent at a distance. Also, they keep you flexible and develop your leg muscles. U.S. kyokushin uses leg and arm techniques in an equal ratio. The blocks, strikes, and punches are very strongly developed. It's a difficult style of karate that will give you a big advantage in close fights where arm techniques are essential.

The karate workout regimen in this book is based primarily upon tae kwon do, and to avoid confusion we will call all our programs "tae kwon do." These programs are set at a beginner's level. Anyone can learn karate at any age. Maybe you won't become a master, but you can learn the techniques set forth in this book. Actually, these basic techniques are the most helpful in actual sparring situations. With this book, you begin your studies. May they never end.

Franz Busen:

I came to tae kwon do because I wanted a more flexible body. Not a more muscular body, a bigger body, or one that was better proportioned. I already had all those attributes, thanks to weight lifting.

After a stint in the army, I had grown fat. Weight lifting and a good diet took care of that. But I had grown muscle-bound because I hadn't paid proper attention to a good stretch regimen.

So off I went to a stretch school, which, by good fortune, also happened to teach tae kwon do. I had never thought of myself as a tense person, but after taking a few tae kwon do classes, I found myself experiencing an incredible release. As you will learn, stretch is an integral part of tae kwon do. In order to perform the techniques properly, you must have an extended body.

When you first begin to stretch, it might not be the most pleasurable experience in the world. But after a few workouts, most people look forward to these exercises. It actually feels good to get the tension out of your body. And when your body feels relaxed, so does your mind. As you stretch, your attention automatically focuses on your body. As a result, the troubles that have built up during the day tend to

Franz.

disappear, or at least take on a secondary importance.

With tae kwon do, you have to concentrate on your body. With weight lifting, I would quite often think about something else—a movie I'd just seen, my studies at school—as I performed the repetitions. This trick would help me to mentally "bypass" the pain, enabling me to do more reps. With tae kwon do, this just isn't possible—the techniques are too difficult. They involve more than just lifting and putting down a big dumbbell. The techniques are intricate maneuvers and demand strong mental concentration. You will have to perform them many times before they become part of your consciousness. The concentration you develop in learning them, however, is good preparation for developing another kind of mental focus, one which is essential for those who are serious about studying tae kwon do. Let me give you an example.

Everyone has seen karate experts break through wood boards with a mere jab of the hand. Well, you won't learn how do *that* from this book. But such a technique does show how mental focus works in order to create a very effective source of power. Every bit of that karate expert's mental focus is concentrated on his hand. He's not thinking about the problem of the day. He's not thinking about what he'll be eating for dinner that night. He's concentrating on his hand hitting that board. It's the difference between driving a sharp stake into a slab of cement and trying to drive a stake with a blunt edge into the same slab of cement. When your focus is sharp and well directed, you can obtain the results you want.

This ability to concentrate doesn't stop when you leave the classroom. I soon found that I could also focus my mind so that I wouldn't worry needlessly about things over which I had no control. Instead, I gave my full attention to what I *could* change. And from there, I got the job done.

Tae kwon do isn't easy. There's no quick way to learn the techniqes, and they are strenuous to perform. Obviously, if you practice tae kwon do regularly, you'll develop your strength. The thing I learned from tae kwon do, however, is that physical strength is not everything when it comes to sparring with an opponent. There are other qualities even more important: alertness, endurance, breath control, and the ability to anticipate an opponent's moves. We call this "developing a good eye."

What started for me as a physical fitness regimen quickly developed into something much, much more. I went on to get my black belt in tae kwon do, and was soon participating in tournaments all over Germany. In the classroom, you generally spar with the same opponents, and you quite often use the same techniques in the same sparring patterns. In a tournament, your opponent is more variable. With him ·or her you encounter new situations, new moves. It's very unpredictable, and you have to focus your concentration even more acutely.

In most tae kwon do tournaments there are three laps, each three minutes long, with one-minute rests in between. It doesn't sound like much, but those three minutes really test your endurance. As your body begins to tire, your mental concentration often loses its focus. This is where most contenders fail. Through training, though, you can acquire the mental discipline to block out the pain of a tired body and continue sparring, your attention undivided.

Today, I am a physical education instructor by profession. Obviously, fitness to me is more than an hour a day at the gym or classroom. Fitness is a way of life, and I firmly believe that it is also a way to change your life. Tae kwon do is exercise. It's also an art, a self-defense program, and a philosophy. You may not be interested in learning all these aspects, but with tae kwon do, they are all there if you want them.

WHAT IS
TAE KWON DO?

1

This karate exercise program is an all-around workout—sports, exercise, self-defense, and even a little philosophy. Tae kwon do can be all of these things—or maybe only one, depending on what you want to derive from this program. Tae kwon do does not promise perfection, but it can help you develop the kind of body and mind you will learn to respect and care for properly. It is certainly not an easy workout regimen in any sense. You will have to exert as much energy mentally as you do physically, if you want to perform the techniques correctly.

To get into shape, people try all kinds of workouts—weight lifting, aerobics, jogging, calisthenics, etc. The promises are never-ending. All you have to do is follow the instructions. It's not even very difficult to convince overweight, out-of-shape people that if they start a new regime, they can get the ultimate body in no time. People are vulnerable. They trust what they are told, and sometimes, after a brief period of working out, they do begin to see some improvement in their bodies. They lose weight. They feel better. So far, so good.

The problem with so many of these exercise programs is that even though they may produce some initial results, the activities involved are rarely varied enough. In time they begin to seem monotonous, routine, even boring. And most important, they do not challenge the mind. In fact, many exercise programs require so little mental concentration that we can daydream about something else while we perform them.

Not so with tae kwon do.

With tae kwon do, you will develop a stronger, healthier, better-defined body; learn the basic skills of self-defense; and develop powers of concentration that can lead to success in other areas of your life.

1. Develop a stronger, healthier, better-defined body. It's important for the human body to have exercise, and proper amounts of it. After a day's work at home or in the office, you begin to feel stress. Your body is exhausted and your pulse rate is way up. Your system suffers because the heart has to beat more times per minute, which is stressful for the heart. The resting pulse can be between 60 and 90 beats per minute. A pulse beat of 60 is excellent, and 70 to 75 is considered normal. Ninety is high, but not dangerous. If you analyze the difference between 60 and 90 beats per minute, you'll see that the heart has to pump the blood 30 times more per minute. In one year, that's about 14,500,000 beats *more* just to live!

Through tae kwon do, you can increase the size and strength of your heart, making it much easier for the organ to do its work. There's no easy way to perform tae kwon do. It's a no-nonsense, tough, and strenuous form of exercise. When you push yourself to the limit during a tae kwon do workout, the regeneration will occur quickly if physical exertion is followed by adequate relaxation. Soon your body will be able to perform more easily, and you will have a greater energy reserve.

As your heart grows stronger with tae kwon do exercises, so do the other muscles of your body. Tae kwon do is a discipline that is learned through the repetition of various techniques which work very specific areas of the body. No part is left out. These repetitions build and define the muscles. And yet, unlike so many other forms of exercise, tae kwon do requires a very limber body in order to perform high kicks and various other techniques. Because you will also be performing a series of highly disciplined stretch programs, you will not feel stiff after a tae kwon do workout. The result is a healthier, more flexible body with highly defined muscle tone.

2. Learn the basic skills of self-defense. Tae kwon do is a highly ritualized form of martial art. Even though this form of karate had its genesis as a kind of self-defense in ancient Korea, the tae kwon do taught in classrooms around the world today is not immediately adaptable to real-life street situations involving

Punching mitts help you to localize your target.

violent persons. In the classroom, tae kwon do is based upon respect for your opponent. In the street, a mugger has no respect. The basic techniques of tae kwon do are the foundation of our self-defense program, but certain adaptations have to be made when you are confronted by an attacker. We will show you how.

3. *Develop powers of concentration.* As we've already stated in our introduction to this book, tae kwon do has given us the power of concentration. In tae kwon do, you must focus upon a single action or technique to the exclusion of everything else—if you want to achieve optimum power. And, of course, we all do. The power and force that can be packed into one gesture are incredible. In tae kwon do you learn how to focus energy so that your concentration is not interrupted by thoughts that can only deter you. Tae

kwon do is a powerful form of karate, and its power begins in the mind.

THE PROGRAMS

The programs in this book are designed to be dynamic and varied. The ten programs include a variety of exercises. Besides tae kwon do techniques, you will find dynamic bodybuilding exercises, calisthenics, and static and dynamic stretches.

Each program is comprised of karate techniques, such as punches, blocks, kicks, and stances. You will build your expertise by following the program in sequence, from one to ten. Because you should begin each workout with a warm-up stretch to prepare the body, we have also included a complete stretching program.

You will also find workout programs on abdominals, self-defense, and katas, which are prearranged fighting patterns. These are optional and depend on how much you want to pursue a particular aspect of this exercise program: general fitness (abdominals), self-defense, or the art of tae kwon do.

EQUIPMENT

It is not necessary to spend a lot of money on equipment. In fact, you can practice tae kwon do without investing a cent in workout aids. There are, however, advantages to owning a few added extras.

Mirror. It is important to watch and control your movements. With a mirror, you will be able to check your techniques with the photographs in this book to see if you are executing them correctly.

Jump rope. Jumping rope is perfect for aerobic training. It warms up the body, builds endurance, and most important for tae kwon do, strengthens the leg muscles.

Punching mitts. Good for such tae kwon do com-

binations as a punch-punch or punch-kick. Mitts will help you to localize your target.

MEDITATION

Before and after each exercise session, you should meditate for two to three minutes. This will relax your mind and body and relieve any stress that has accumulated during the day. Meditation is important because it lets you set aside emotional upsets or problems that can prevent you from working out to your potential. If you are wrapped up in a personal matter that happened a few hours earlier, your concentration is compromised. Meditation lets you focus your energies exclusively on a particular goal, is this case, your workout.

Although certain Eastern philosophies have made meditation into a very difficult and exotic activity, it is really quite simple. To begin, kneel comfortably, close your eyes, and make a tight fist. Relax your shoulders as you push out your chest. Remove every negative thought from your mind. Think pleasant and soothing thoughts for 30 to 45 seconds, then clear your mind completely. With your last minute of meditation, focus on how you would like to look. This will help you to begin the exercises with a receptive and willing attitude. (Of course you can meditate as long as you wish, but do meditate at least two to three minutes.)

After the workout, sit down and relax your mind and body again. Ask yourself if you performed to your capacity. Did you meet your goals?

Meditation: Every tae kwon do program begins and ends with a relaxation of the mind and body.

STRETCH PROGRAM

Yes, we have included an extensive stretch program along with our tae kwon do instructions. These stretches are not incidental to our martial arts program, but rather an integral part of it, for two major reasons:

1. Without a flexible body, you simply cannot perform all the tae kwon do moves. A certain degree of stretch, or extension, is required.

2. Tae kwon do is a strenuous martial arts program, and it can lead to injury if your body is not properly warmed up before practice. "Warm-up" refers to the temperature of the body. The body must be at a certain temperature before it can participate in rigorous activity of any kind. Stretching the body is the only way of getting the blood to the muscles to prepare them for the workout to come. In its natural state the body is tense, stiff. Muscles need to be warmed up before the power inherent in them can be transformed into strength and speed.

Tae kwon do involves strenuous exercise. If you do not perform stretches before and after the core workout, tae kwon do can leave your body even more stiff and tense than it was prior to working out. Because they release tension, stretches help prevent your body from becoming injured. However, these exercises can also hurt the body if they are executed improperly. So there is one rule to follow: Never start with difficult stretches. If you do, pulled muscles and tendons can occur. Go easy. Get to know your body. In the beginning, it's better not to challenge yourself with difficult exercises. Don't push. Feel the resistance in your body, but don't force it. There's no reason to overdo it and then spend valuable time recovering from soreness or worse, a serious injury.

Stretch exercises help you to:

1. Avoid injury.
2. Prepare the body for the more rigorous activity to come.

3. Enhance concentration.
4. Improve flexibility.
5. Release tension.
6. Gain coordination.

To achieve all six of these goals, we recommend that you incorporate four different stretch sessions in your stretch program. Each session contains the two basic types of stretches—static and dynamic.

Static stretching occurs without muscle contractions. You bring your body to a described position, and without moving or bouncing, hold it there for approximately eight counts. The purpose of static stretching is the extension of tendons, which will give you a good all-around flexibility.

Static stretches should always be followed by a series of *dynamic stretches*. After your tendons and muscles have been stretched by static exercises, they are then ready for an active workout involving gently bouncing movements. Some exercise trainers refer to bounces as "pulses," a term which connotes a much smaller, more controlled movement. Whichever term is used, they are very small beats that, one after the other, gradually increase the stretch in your body. A bounce gently pushes your limbs so that you feel a greater degree of resistance in them. For example, if we recommend that you bounce 10 times, you should increase the stretch slightly with each bounce. With bounce number 10, you should feel greater resistance in your body than you did with the first one. Obviously, this cannot be achieved if you simply bounce your limbs without any thought of control. The important thing here is to push the limbs, feel the resistance, then let up slightly. Push more the next time, feel the resistance again, and let up slightly—but not as much as you did the first time. And so on, increasing the resistance very, very slightly with each bounce. Dynamic stretches will make your muscles more responsive, enabling them to react quickly without undue strain.

Together, static and dynamic stretches will provide an adequate all-around warm-up. We have combined them here in four stretch sessions to be performed before, during, and after each tae kwon do program. These sessions are first described briefly, then outlined step by step.

1. Warm-up stretch. Designed to improve your general flexibility. It takes about 15 to 20 minutes to complete all the exercises in this session. This is our longest stretch workout because it initiates your body to the more strenuous tae kwon do techniques to come. Each of the programs starts with the warm-up stretch.

2. Conditioning stretch. Performed during or after a tae kwon do program. Never start with this set of stretches. They are too strenuous and by themselves will not warm up the body. This session is quickly performed—8 to 10 minutes—and will increase your endurance by bringing the body to a rapid physical peak.

3. Cool-down stretch. Always performed after your complete tae kwon do workout. It will slowly reduce your body temperature and pulse rate. Tense muscles and tendons will also be eased, letting them relax so that you will not experience soreness later. The session takes about five minutes to perform.

4. Relax stretch. Performed during a tae kwon do program. After executing some of the more strenuous tae kwon do moves, this session will give you a welcome break in which to recover, collect energy, and concentrate on a specific area of your body that has perhaps been overworked.

The relax stretch involves active relaxation exercises that can be performed as needed during the other stretch sessions. Because certain exercises tense your muscles and tendons, it is necessary to relax them before you continue your workout. During any strenuous physical workout, your blood pressure and pulse frequently are pushed up. At some point, you will reach a physical peak, shortly after which exhaustion sets in. It is detrimental to your heart simply to take an abrupt, passive rest. You have to bring down your pulse frequency gradually. Performing the relax stretch guarantees this gradual decrease.

RELAX STRETCH BREATHING

The relax stretch regimen involves a special breathing technique, which is easy to perform. Extend your arms and inhale deeply through your nose. While inhaling, lead palms to your ribs without touching them. Keep palms up. Hold your breath for half a second. Now, breathe out from your diaphragm through your mouth and nose, pushing out as much air as possible. While you are breathing out, tense your arms and upper body and turn palms to the floor, pushing your arms down to your sides. Each time you inhale repeat this procedure.

After reaching a physical peak, your body is soon exhausted. But proper breathing helps your system to regenerate quickly. That's why it's important to exhale as much and as strongly as possible, because the more you exhale, the more you can inhale. The more you inhale, the more oxygen you can bring into your body and the faster you regenerate.

Even more important, this special breathing technique helps you to focus your concentration so that you don't allow your body to collapse. Despite physical exhaustion, your mind and your eyes are still strong, waiting to give the body their command. They tell the body which move is necessary. Properly controlled breathing is the easiest way to obtain the concentration you need to overcome this momentary exhaustion.

On the following pages each stretch session is outlined in detail.

Breathing technique for the relax stretch: 1) Extend arms, 2) inhale deeply leading hands to ribs, 3) exhale turning palms to floor. See "Relax Stretch Breathing," page 25.

A. WARM-UP STRETCH

The warm-up stretch is just that: It warms up your body and must be performed before any other kind of exercise workout, whether that be the tae kwon do programs, conditioning stretch, or the katas.

1. *Jump in place: a.* Jump in place with legs closed, 20 times. *b.* Jumping jacks with hands on hips, 20 times. *c.* Bring left knee to chest, then return left foot to floor. Ten times each leg.

2. *Ankle circles:* Raise right knee to groin level and circle right foot five times clockwise, five times counterclockwise. Shake leg and lower to floor. Raise left knee and repeat exercise with left foot.

1.c

3. *Knee bends:* Put heels together with feet at 45-degree angle. Do not let heels come off the floor, and keep knees in line over toes. Bend knees and straighten, five times. Put feet together, parallel. Bend knees and straighten, five times.

4. *Knee circles:* Put hands on knees and rotate knees in a circle, keeping heels on floor. Five times clockwise, five times counterclockwise.

5. *Hip circles:* With feet shoulder width apart, put hands on hips and rotate hips in a circle, keeping knees slightly bent. Five times clockwise, five times counterclockwise.

6. *Waist reaches:* Feet shoulder width apart, reach with left arm over head to right side, push with right hand on right hip to left side. Hold for five counts (static stretch), two times on each side. Then bounce five times (dynamic stretch), two times on each side. See photo, page 23.

7. *Trunk twists:* With hands behind head and feet shoulder width apart, turn upper body back to your right and then to the left. Hold for five counts (static stretch), two times on each side. Then bounce three times (dynamic stretch), two times on each side.

8. *Static combination stretch: a.* Feet slightly more than shoulder width apart, let head hang loosely between legs. Feel resistance in tendons. Hold five counts. *b.* Same foot position as in *a.* Hold hands together and lead them over head as far as possible, arching back. Hold five counts.

9. *Dynamic combination stretch:* Repeat 8 *a* and *b*, except this time bounce as you stretch. Bounce 10 times each side.

10. *Arm circles:* Feet shoulder width apart, extend arms straight out from your sides. Rotate arms 10 times forward, 10 back.

11. *Head turns:* Bring chin to chest, then let head fall back, five times up and down. Bring chin over left shoulder, then bring it over right, five times left and right.

12. *Head rolls:* Circle head clockwise five times, then counterclockwise five times.

13.a

13.b

13.c

13. *Static hamstring and spine stretch series: a.* Feet double shoulder width apart. Hold left ankle or calf and pull upper body to knee. Keep legs straight. Hold for eight counts. Now repeat with right leg. *b.* Grab both ankles and pull your chest to your knees. Hold for eight counts. *c.* Rise from position in *b*. Put hands on hips and push hips forward. Hold for eight counts.

14.a

14.b

14. *Static jazz stretch: a.* Lunge with right foot forward. Stretch out left leg behind you. Back foot is flat on floor at a 45-degree angle, front foot points straight ahead. Put hands on right thigh and keep upper body erect. Now, push left hip down. Hold for eight counts. Repeat on left side. *b.* Same position as *a*, except that with the back foot only the ball of foot touches the floor. Hold eight counts. Repeat on other side. *c.* Same position as *b*. Twist upper body back to right side with arms swung out at hip level. Look to your left heel. Hold eight counts on each side.

14.c

17.

18.

15. *Dynamic hamstring and spine stretch series: a.* Place legs far enough apart that you feel a slight resistance or stretch between them. Hold left ankle or calf and pull upper body to knee. Now bounce gently, five times over each knee. *b.* Legs slightly more apart. Grab both ankles and pull yourself down. Keep legs straight. Bounce gently for eight counts. *c.* Legs as wide as possible. Rise from position in *b.* Put hands on hips and push hips forward. Bounce eight times.

16. *Dynamic jazz stretch series:* Repeat the static jazz stretch series (exercises 14 *a, b,* and *c*). Bounce instead of hold as you stretch.

17. *Groin stretch:* Feet shoulder width apart. Assume a squat position with your buttocks almost, but not quite, touching the floor. Triceps of arms touch inside of knees. Now bring hips forward an inch by slightly pushing knees to outside. Twenty times.

18. *Side squat stretch:* In a squat position, stretch out left leg to the side, flexing foot. Keep weight on right leg and place hands in front of you on the floor. Bounce 10 times. Repeat on right side.

19. PERFORM RELAX STRETCH BREATHING TECHNIQUE. See pages 25–26.

20. *Chinese split series: a.* Legs double shoulder width apart (until you feel resistance), feet flat on floor pointing straight forward, hands on hips. Hold for eight counts. *b.* Same position as *a.* Bend upper torso down between legs, keeping back flat. Grab your calves or ankles. Bounce eight times. *c.* Same position as *b.* Place hands on floor in front of you for support. Try to stretch legs as far apart as possible. Hold for eight counts. *d.* Same position as *c.* See-saw hips five times forward and five times back. *e.* Same position as *c.* Move forward with hands and push hips toward floor. Bounce 10 times. *f.* Same position as *e.* Twist right and left hips, alternating up and down toward floor. Bounce five times each side. *g.* Out of last position (*f*), spread legs as wide as possible and put knees on floor. Now, push hips down to floor. Ten times.

20.a

20.c

20.e

20.g

21. *Spine stretch in push-up position:* Fall into push-up position, feet shoulder width apart. Now, push hips down to floor while looking up at ceiling, chin back. Bounce 10 times.

22. *Calf stretch:* Out of position 21, put legs together and push buttocks up until you feel resistance in calfs. (Body should form a triangle with buttocks at apex.) Now walk in place, leaving balls of feet on the floor and moving only your heels so that you feel resistance. Ten times each leg.

23. *Static Korean split: a.* Sit down, open legs as wide as possible, and flex toes. Place right hand in front of you, left hand behind buttocks. Push yourself up two inches off the floor and push hips forward to right hand. Feet do not move. Hold for 10 seconds. Return to sitting position. Five times. *b.* Bring chest to left thigh and grab ankle or foot. Keep head up. Hold for eight counts. Repeat on other side. *c.* Bring chest to center between legs. Look straight forward and place hands behind head. Hold for eight counts.

24. *Dynamic Korean split:* Same positions as 23 *b* and *c.* Bounce 10 times in each position.

25. *Frog split series: a.* Sit down, your upper body erect. Put heels together, grab ankles, and bring buttocks to heels. Bounce knees up and down 20 times. *b.* Same position as *a.* Grab ankles, put elbows on calfs and push down. Bounce 10 times. *c.* Same position as *a.* Pull head down to heels. Bounce 10 times.

21.

23.a

25. b

27.

26. *Sitting calf stretch:* Sitting, bring your legs together straight out in front of you. Grab toes and lift them off the floor until you feel resistance in calfs. Bounce 10 times.

27. *Half hurdle stretch:* Sitting on floor, place left leg out straight in front of you. Bring sole of right foot to left inner thigh. Grab left foot with both hands. Now, keeping back as flat as possible, pull chest to left leg. Bounce 10 times. Repeat with other leg.

28. *Back stretch series: a.* Lie down on back. Legs together, bring them up over your head and let feet touch the floor behind you. Hands on floor at your side for support. Keep legs straight. Bounce on balls of feet 10 times. *b.* Keep legs together over head. Now, walk legs from right to left. Five times to each side. *c.* Same position. Roll down onto lower back, bringing straight legs up over head. Grab ankles and try to spread legs as far apart as possible. Bounce torso 10 times. *d.* Bring legs together and lower to floor. Touch head to knees. Bounce 10 times.

29. *Thigh stretch series: a.* Take hurdle sit position (left leg straight forward, right leg to the side with right thigh and right calf at a 90-degree angle). Place hands on floor at your sides for support. Now, as you bounce your torso forward, gently spread your thighs farther apart in order to feel the resistance, or stretch, in your groin. Bounce 10 times. *b.* Same position. Left leg straight, head to left knee. Bounce 10 times. *c.* Same position. Head to right knee. Bounce 10 times. *d.* Same position. Arch back and try to touch shoulders to floor. Bounce 10 times. *e.* Repeat sequence with right leg straight forward, left leg bent to the side.

28.a

28.c

29.a

30.

30. *Gym split:* Out of Chinese split, extend back leg and raise body so that your buttocks are no longer resting on the floor. Place both hands on floor, one hand on each side of your body for support. Bounce torso over each knee 10 times.

31. *Korean thigh stretch:* Kneel on floor. Grab ankles and slowly lower back to floor. Feel resistance in thighs.

31.

32. *Final relax stretch: a.* Jump in place for 10 seconds. Keeping legs shoulder width apart, execute the following: *b.* Hip circles, 10 times in each direction. *c.* Waist reaches, 10 times. *d.* Push hips forward, 10 times. *e.* Arm circles, 10 times in each direction. *f.* Head rolls, five times in each direction.

33. *Leg swings: a.* Put right hand on wall or chair for support. Now lift left leg to the side of your torso. Seven times each side. *b.* Put right hand on chair and rest left hand on hip. Swing left leg to the front and back. Keep leg straight. Ten times each side.

33.b

B. CONDITIONING STRETCH

The conditioning stretch is performed during or after a tae kwon do workout, as indicated in the text. Never execute the conditioning stretch prior to beginning a tae kwon do workout or any other strenuous form of exercise. Unlike the warm-up stretch, the conditioning stretch is too rigorous to be used as an introductory, or warm-up, stretch.

1. *Jump in place: a.* Jump with legs closed, 15 times. *b.* Jumping jacks, 15 times. *c.* Jog in place, 30 times. *d.* Bring left knee to chest, 15 times. Repeat with right leg. *e.* Bring left knee to side of chest, 15 times. Repeat with right leg. *f.* Bring heel of left leg to buttocks, 15 times. Repeat with right leg.

2. *Groin jump:* Feet shoulder width apart. Fall into a squat position with your buttocks almost, but not quite, touching the floor.

With hands behind head, jump up and down. Legs, of course, never completely straighten. Exhale jumping up, inhale coming down. Fifteen times.

3. *Dynamic leg lifts: a.* Sit on floor, placing hands behind back. Left leg is bent, right leg straight. Now lift hips and raise right leg straight up, toes flexed. Lower leg to an inch off floor. Raise leg on a one-second count, lower leg on a three-second count. Repeat 10 times with each leg. *b.* Same position. This time lift leg to side. Ten times each leg.

4. PERFORM RELAX STRETCH BREATHING TECHNIQUE FOLLOWED BY GYM SPLIT STRETCH (A. 30).

5. *Push-up position stretches:* Leg clasps. Take a push-up position on the floor with your feet together. Now, "walk" the feet out to the side until they are double shoulder width apart, then walk them back together. Repeat 20 times. *b.* Push-ups. Perform as many as you can, keeping back straight.

6. PERFORM RELAX STRETCH BREATHING TECHNIQUE FOLLOWED BY GYM SPLIT STRETCH (A. 30).

3.a

7.a

7.b

7. *Speed kick (thigh strengthener):* Stand with legs shoulder width apart, hands on hips. *a.* Stretch right foot back, keeping both knees bent, right knee almost touching floor. Left foot is pointed straight ahead with only ball of right foot touching the floor. *b.* Out of this position, kick forward with right leg as fast as possible. (As you will later learn, this is called a front snap kick.) Return to starting position. Twenty-five times on each side.

8. PERFORM RELAX STRETCH BREATHING TECHNIQUE FOLLOWED BY GYM SPLIT STRETCH (A. 30).

9. *Calf strengthener:* Feet double shoulder width apart, pointed straight ahead. Hands on hips and upper torso erect. Lift only your heels off the floor and put them back down. Fifty times.

10. *Final pyramid series:*
First series—a. Speed kick, 20 times; *b.* Sit-ups, 20 times; *c.* Push-ups, 20 times.
Second series—a. Speed kick, 15 times; *b.* Sit-ups, 15 times; *c.* Push-ups, 15 times.
Third series—a. Speed kick, 10 times; *b.* Sit-ups, 10 times; *c.* Push-ups, 10 times.
Note: The final pyramid series is designed to build endurance and

strength, and should be performed without break between exercises. When performing sit-ups, it is necessary to observe a few precautions in order to avoid lower-back strain. Keep knees bent and feet on floor at all times. Hands are held behind the head. Touch head to knees. When lowering torso, do not arch the back or let your head or shoulders touch the floor.

11. PERFORM RELAX STRETCH BREATHING TECHNIQUE FOLLOWED BY GYM SPLIT STRETCH (A. 30).

C. COOL-DOWN STRETCH

The cool-down stretch is performed after a tae kwon do workout, or any other type of strenuous exercise. Do not use the cool-down stretch as an introductory stretch; it relaxes instead of warms up the body.

1. *Knee bends* (see stretch A.3): 10 times.

2. *Knee circles* (see stretch A.4): five times each direction.

3. *Hip circles* (see stretch A.5): five times each direction.

4. *Waist reaches* (see stretch A.6): five times each direction.

5. *Hip releases:* Take push-up position. Left leg remains straight as left foot rests on outer instep. Put right foot behind left heel, extend arms all the way out, and twist your left hip to floor. Ten times each side.

6. *Spine release:* Push-up position, legs shoulder width apart. Look to ceiling and bounce hips up and down slightly. Ten times.

7. *Dynamic Korean split series:* (See stretch A. 24). Bounce 10 times in each position.

8. *Sit-ups:* Put your feet under a sofa. Bend legs so that they make a 45-degree angle with chest. Now lie on back, hands behind head, and sit up on a two-second count. When going back, head and shoulders do not touch floor. Go back on a five-second count. Ten times.

9. MEDITATE 1-2 MINUTES.

D. RELAX STRETCH

The relax stretch is performed during tae kwon do workouts in order to give your body needed rests. Simply to cease exercising all together, however, is potentially harmful. Instead, the relax stretch continues your exercise program while bringing your pulse rate down.

1. *Jog easily in place:* 15 seconds, or until pulse rate decreases.

2. *Shake legs and arms:* 10 seconds.

3. *Special breathing technique:* See pages 25–26 for instructions.

4. *Hip release:* Lie on back, arms on floor for support. Bring legs over head, touching toes to floor behind head. Twist hips to right and left side, keeping legs straight. Ten times.

5. *Lie on floor:* Close eyes for 15 seconds. Control breathing and try to regain concentration.

5.

ABDOMINAL PROGRAM

3

Strong abdominal muscles are essential for performing tae kwon do. Of course, a flat, taut stomach *looks* great too. But in tae kwon do, strong abdominals also serve a very specific purpose.

Since tae kwon do stances are performed with bent knees, the natural tendency is to strike a stance and then let the weight of the body fall into the knees. In a normal standing position, the knees are straight or only slightly bent, meaning the pressure is placed elsewhere. But as soon as the knees bend, pressure tends to focus in the knees. After a long period of time, this can result in fatigue, if not injury to the knees. The only way to take pressure off the knees in a bent-knee position is to give the body a "lift." Here is where strong abdominals come into play.

In tae kwon do, the knees are almost always bent while the back remains erect. And for good reason. The torso is straight so that the abdominal muscles can pull the weight up, preventing it from "settling" into the knees. It is not enough merely to tense the stomach muscles upon striking a stance. The muscles must also be trained to lift the body.

How is this done?

Turn profile in a mirror and tense, or tighten, your abdominal muscles. Do they protrude as much as or even more than they did before you tensed them? If so, trying tensing them again. This time give your abdomen and stomach a slightly concave profile. At the same time, make sure that your back remains flat. Do not hunch over. You should feel a stretch or pulling upward in your stomach. Also, your chest should rise slightly as a result. This is the "lift" we talked about earlier.

As your abdominals grow stronger, the more lift you will be able to attain and the less pressure you will feel in your knees.

There are two kinds of abdominal exercises: *static* and *dynamic*, in other words, those which involve bounces (dynamic) and those which do not (static). Both are necessary for building strong muscles. There are, however, two different ways to develop abdominal muscles. The first approach is to increase the number of repetitions. The second involves performing fewer reps, but making the exercises more difficult by adding weights. The first approach is especially good for burning away fat rolls, while the second tends to produce larger, less well defined muscles. It's a question of aesthetics, and the choice is yours.

For the abdominal exercises, we have set the number of repetitions at a beginner's level. If you find that you can perform more repetitions than are given here, then do so. Always push yourself. You are working out for yourself, and no one else. Ideally, this abdominal program should be executed every day; less than twice a week, however, and the results will be minimal.

1.

2.

1. *Sofa sit-ups* (upper abdominals): Lie flat on your back with knees together and bent at a 45-degree angle. For support, feet are held underneath the sofa, hands are behind head. Raise chin to knees on a two-second count, then lower upper body to starting position on a five-second count. In order to prevent back strain, do not let head or shoulders touch floor upon return to starting position. Ten reps, two sets, with a 30-second rest between sets.

Note: After each abdominal exercise, relax your abdominal muscles by taking the push-up position. Push your hips toward the floor as you look up to the ceiling. Bounce your hips gently. (See photo 21, page 32.)

2. *Bent leg raises* (lower abdominals): Sit on floor and place hands beside buttocks for support. Lift legs two inches off the floor and bring knees over navel on a two-second count. Return legs to starting position on a five-second count. Do not let legs touch floor. Ten reps, two sets, with a 30-second rest between sets.

3. *Rear flutters* (back muscles and upper abdominals): Lie flat on stomach with arms and legs stretched out. Lift arms and legs into a V-formation and hold for five seconds. Now, on a five-second count, lower legs and arms but do not let them touch the floor. Ten reps, two sets, with a 30-second rest between sets.

4. *Twisting crunches* (lower, upper, and side abdominals): Lie flat on floor with hands behind head. Lift legs and shoulders two inches off the floor. Now, raise right knee over navel and bring left elbow to it. Return elbow and leg to off-floor position and repeat the exercise with left leg and right elbow. Perform this exercise as fast as possible. Ten reps, two sets, with a one-minute rest between sets.

5. *Killer holds* (abdominals and deltoids): Position two chairs so far apart that when you place your hands on one seat and your feet on the other, your body is completely stretched out. Hold for five seconds.

4.

5.

7.

8.a

8.b

6. *Buttocks raises* (buttocks and middle abdominals): Lie flat on floor and, with your knees together and bent, raise buttocks as high as possible, keeping your feet, arms, and shoulders on the floor for support. Slowly lower and raise buttocks. Ten times, two reps, with a one-minute rest between sets.

7. *Crunches* (upper abdominals): Lie flat on floor with hands behind head. Put legs on chair and fix a point on the ceiling directly overhead. Now bring shoulders as far off the floor as possible while lower back remains on floor; keep looking at the same point, and hold for five counts. Lower shoulders to the floor. Repeat five times, five counts each.

8. *Bent leg raises* (lower abdominals): Lie flat on back with knees together and legs two inches off floor. Get a firm grip on sofa or chair. *a.* Bring knees into chest, *b.* then straighten them up, creating a 90-degree angle with your torso. Slowly lower legs to floor, but do not let them touch. Ten times, three sets, with a one-minute rest between sets.

TAE KWON DO
PROGRAMS

4

The martial arts programs we have developed are based on tae kwon do, but, as we explained earlier, they also incorporate some techniques from a style of Japanese karate called kyokushin. Tae kwon do and kyokushin are only two of the many schools of karate. Over the centuries, these different schools have borrowed certain basic techniques from one another, and yet each has its own distinctive focus, particularly with regard to where the emphasis of attack is placed—the legs or the hands. In most schools of Japanese karate, including kyokushin, hand techniques tend to predominate. After all, karate means "empty hand." Tae kwon do, the Korean style, places the emphasis on leg techniques. In fact, the focus of tae kwon do is about 70 percent leg techniques, 30 percent hand. Even though our program is basically tae kwon do, we have added a few punches and blocks from the kyokushin school in order to make the workout more well-rounded, not only for purposes of physical fitness, but of self-defense as well.

In a close fight, hand techniques (punches and blocks) are very important. The proximity of an aggressor is usually extremely intimate, and the space needed to perform leg techniques (kicks) is often simply not available. Hand techniques are also very practical in that they are relatively easier to learn than kicks, particularly high kicks. Clearly, kicks are more powerful, and they are most effective at keeping a distance between you and your opponent. These techniques, however, require a degree of flexibility in your legs that is usually achieved only through extensive tae kwon do training, including stretching.

No one ever said tae kwon do would be easy. Because it emphasizes leg techniques that work the entire body, tae kwon do is a tough, strenuous exercise regimen that can leave the body exhausted. But you get back what you put into it.

KEY CONCEPTS

Unlike jogging or aerobic dance, karate is a highly ritualized, intensely defined form of exercise. There is a correct and an incorrect way to perform even the smallest gesture. The following points will help you find the correct way.

Repetitions

These programs are built upon repetitions of exercises and techniques. As with other exercise programs, these repetitions build strength and endurance. In tae kwon do, however, they are also a unique part of the learning process with a special purpose. After a certain period of training, you will no longer have to think how to perform a specific hand or leg technique. Having repeated it frequently in practice, you will develop a natural and automatic behavior of defense. In the classroom or on the street, you will be able to defend yourself without having to think about which punch or kick to use. You will know and respond on reflex.

Stances

A stance is a position from which techniques are delivered. We have included five stances in our martial-arts program. They are the ready stance, forward stance, back stance, horse stance, and fighting stance. Each stance requires a highly stylized posture: Your upper body remains erect and your legs are bent at all times. This is how tae kwon do is practiced. In an actual fight or sparring match, of course, you would not move in a bent-knee position at all times. You would adapt to the circumstances and react accordingly. The purpose of training in low stances is to build up strength in your legs to achieve a powerful kick. You also will improve your balance.

If a stance is executed properly, it assures excellent balance. Without balance, your kicks and punches will be ineffectual. They might even miss their targets. In order to move correctly in a stance, a few basic rules should be remembered:

1. All stances are taken with the knees bent and the feet at least shoulder width apart. This lowers your center of gravity, which helps to ensure proper balance.

2. While the bent-knee position lowers your body, abdominal muscles must help to lift it. This is a difficult concept, but let us explain: Imagine a string pulling from the middle of your head through to your navel. Feel it pulling you up as your knees take your body down. To lift your body, never let the string slacken. Keep it taut, and you're on your way to developing great balance.

3. While moving forward and back in a stance, keep your head on one level. The body should not rise and fall dramatically regardless of the punches or kicks delivered. (See "Moving in forward stance" on p. 55.)

Turns

Some tae kwon do techniques are delivered with your feet flat on the floor. Others are practiced as you travel across the floor. Those techniques which travel are practiced in a certain sequence: five times forward, turn, and then five times back. In practice, the starting position is usually a left stance. For example, if you walk in forward stance, you would always start with your left leg in front. *a.* You would end in right forward stance. *b.* To turn, shift your weight onto right leg, cross arms in front, and move your left leg behind your body to the right so that your feet are shoulder width apart. Your right foot remains flat on the floor while only the ball of your left foot touches the floor. *c.* Now turn your body 180 degrees to the back, shifting your weight onto your left leg. (The turn itself must be executed on the balls of your feet.) Then throw your arms down to hip level. You will end in left forward stance, ready to put your right foot forward into right forward stance.

Turns: a.   **b.**   **c.**

Breathing

As we discussed earlier, proper breathing has a special meaning in tae kwon do training. It relaxes and calms you. Even more significantly, breathing can help to control your mind by allowing you to focus your attention in spite of physical exhaustion.

You should always inhale after you have executed a move. Exhale when you apply a punch or kick. This will make your move more powerful, and because the exhalation of breath automatically relaxes your muscles, it will prevent an opponent's blow from inflicting undue harm.

Shock and Snap Effects

All tae kwon do techniques are executed in a special way. Hand techniques, such as the forefist punch or the high block, have to be performed with a shock. This effect is achieved by a turning of either your arms or your wrists. While delivering a punch, the fist you intend to hit with travels straight forward to the target. The other fist is pulled back with the *same velocity*. Both fists nearly touch each other as the one leads forward and the other pulls back. Then, just before reaching their final positions, both fists are turned 180 degrees. (See the "Forefist Punch" on page 57.) By turning both fists at the very last moment, you gain the shock effect which gives your punch an additional force.

The same principle is true when performing a

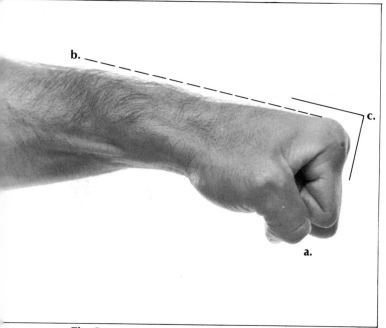

The fist.

block. By turning your wrists at the last moment, you give a shock effect to your technique.

The snap effect, which applies to all kicks, serves a similar purpose. It can be compared to the snapping forward and back motion of a whip. To explain how the effect works in tae kwon do, let's look at the front snap kick, which you will learn in Program 1.

a. Raise your knee to the front at hip level. From this position, *b.* snap your foreleg forward (as you simultaneously push your hip forward) and *c.* back. Through the hip movement you put your body weight into the kick, giving it added power. (See the "Front Snap Kick at groin level" on page 56.)

The Fist

A strong fist is necessary not only for a good punch, but also for avoiding injury, i.e., broken fingers and sprained wrists. A strong fist depends more on how you make it than on sheer muscle. As you might expect, there is a special procedure for making a fist in tae kwon do.

Open your hand, leaving the fingers together. Now, roll them into your palm with the fingertips touching your calluses. Roll them as tightly as possible. *a.* Lock your fingers by putting your thumb on the forefinger and middle finger.

b. In the final fist position, the back of your fist has to be in one straight line with your forearm. *c.* Your fist must build a 90-degree angle in order to be able to hit with your two knuckles, which is the area of impact.

Hitting Areas/Blocking Areas

When you deliver a kick, block, or punch, you should imagine making contact with your opponent with specific areas of your foot, arm or fist. These areas of impact are very defined and must be taken into consideration if you want to give your technique optimum power. Each technique, of course, utilizes a different part of the body.

a. Punch: first two knuckles
b. High/low block: inside of forearm
c. Middle inside block: outside of forearm
d. Front snap kick: balls of feet
e. Roundhouse kick: top of foot
f. Side kick: side of foot
g. Back kick: side of heel
h. Knee kick: knee

Hitting/blocking areas:

a.

b.

c.

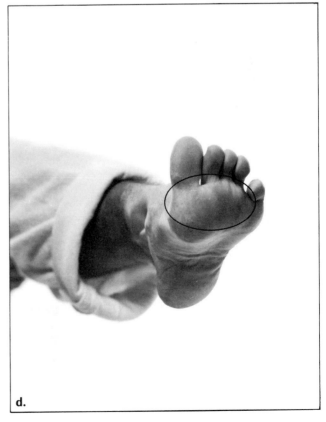

d.

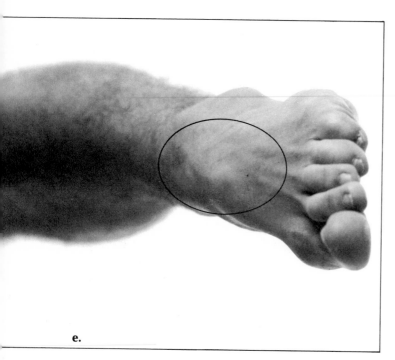

e.

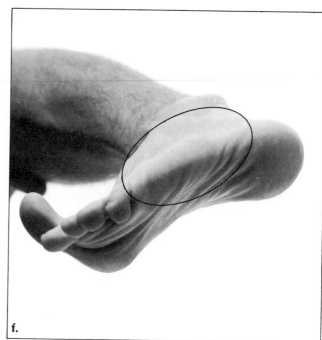

f.

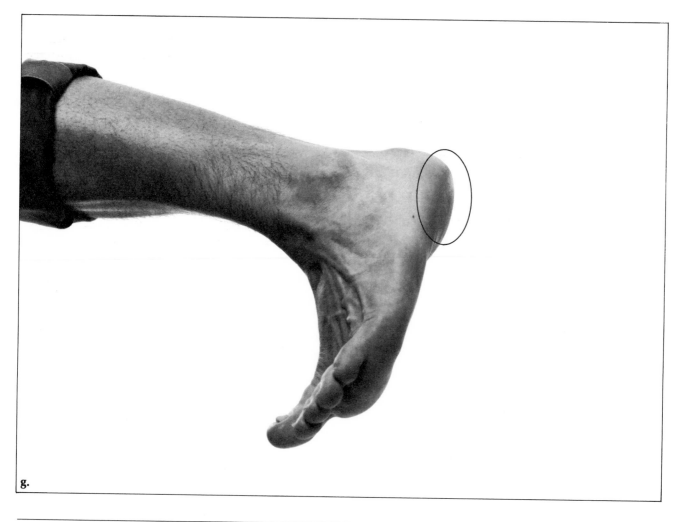

g.

Imaginary Target

Tae kwon do is always practiced with an imaginary opponent. Depending upon the technique performed, you should direct a punch or kick at a specific target on the body of your imaginary opponent. For example, when you execute a high kick, the target would be the face of your imaginary opponent. A low kick would have to be aimed at his groin or knees.

The imaginary opponent is more important than it might seem at first. In tae kwon do, concentration is paramount. Without it, your energy and strength dissipate. The imaginary opponent gives you a focal point to direct your moves and your energy. It helps you concentrate. Having to imagine someone in front of you while you practice will also give you confi-

h.

dence in an actual fight. These techniques—the stances, the kicks, the blocks, and the punches—are not just a dance. They have a purpose and they are directed *at* someone. By imagining the opponent in practice, you will be ready for an opponent in actual combat, whether that takes place in the classroom or on the street. The advantage of control will be yours.

Combinations

Tae kwon do techniques are put together in a number of exercise sequences called "combinations." These combinations show you how to combine one move with another, how to follow a block with a punch or a kick, and how you fall out of a kick into your next stance. They are your basic fighting patterns. After a certain number of repetitions, these combinations will become automatic and you will be able to react upon reflex without thinking which move is next.

Katas

Katas are prearranged fighting patterns which contain a series of combinations. Obviously, they are performed over a much longer duration than just one combination.

REPETITIONS

The first few programs are geared to a beginner's endurance level. The repetitions of exercises are held low. If you find the programs too difficult, we recommend that you simply lower the number of repetitions. However, before moving on to the next program, you should be able to complete the exercises of the previous program with relative ease at the repetition level we have set, because each program builds upon techniques learned in the previous program. One program has to be mastered before you can move on to the next.

Before starting a program, read all the instructions very carefully. Try to remember the given instructions so that you can follow the exercises without having to take long breaks rereading the instructions. Each of the programs will take about 50 minutes to complete. *Very important:* Do not skip the stretch and abdominal programs, which are incorporated in the overall tae kwon do exercises. They serve to prepare and strengthen the body. Without them, you risk possible injury.

PROGRAM 1

The stances, kicks, and punches introduced in our first program are anything but difficult. In fact, you may find them too easy. Mere performance, however, is not the object of Program 1.

Through repetition of these moves, you will learn control and develop a sense of your center. Your balance will improve. Without balance, there can be no power to your movements.

Through repetition you will also develop strength and endurance. Try performing a simple kick just once or twice. You feel nothing. Perform it 10 times, however, and you will begin to feel your body at work. Concentrate on that feeling and you will come to know your body. Concentrate on that feeling to the exclusion of everything else, and you will begin to understand the importance of focusing your attention in tae kwon do. With martial arts, we do not live in the past or the future. If your concentration is total, only the present moment exists—and all of your energy must be focused upon it in order to achieve optimum power.

A. MEDITATION

B. STRETCHES

1.0 *Warm-up stretch:* As with every program, this one begins with stretch exercises. For Program 1, it is recommended that you begin with the Warm-Up Stretch, as shown on pages 26–36. These are elementary exercises that will stretch the body, not strain it. If your body is unconditioned, go easy with these stretches. There's no reason to overextend yourself the first day, and then to be too sore to work out for the next week.

C. ABDOMINALS

See pages 43–45 for instructions.

2.0

D. NEW TECHNIQUES

2.0 *Ready stance:* This stance is used for practice sessions or at the beginning and end of each kata. Hold fists at waist level a few inches in front of you. Feet are shoulder width apart and slightly turned out with knees slightly bent. Practice the ready stance by assuming your normal posture and then falling into this one very slowly.

3.0

3.0 *Forward stance (in place):* With legs shoulder width apart, stretch left leg back and bend the right. Left foot turns out at 45 degrees while right foot is pointed straight ahead. Bend arms and hold fists at hip level, keeping upper body erect. This is the right forward stance. Fall into it five times, then fall into the left forward stance. Practice five times, then fall into right forward stance and repeat the sequence.

3.1 *Moving in forward stance: a.* Begin in left forward stance. Fists at hip level. *b.* Now, slide your right leg next to left, keeping legs bent. *c.* Step forward with right foot into right forward stance. Move five times forward, turn, and then back. Turn after five times. (For the correct turning procedure, see page 49.) *Important:* As you move from one stance to another, your head does not bob up and down, but remains at one level.

3.1a

3.1b

3.1c

4.0 *Front snap kick (groin level): a. and b.* Out of ready stance, raise right thigh to hip level in front so that thigh and calf make a right angle. *c.* Now, let foreleg snap forward, hitting your imaginary target with ball of foot. Toes and foot are flexed. (*Important:* When snapping leg forward, also push hip forward.) Keep leg up in stretched position for half a second, *d.* then pull foreleg back to right angle calf-thigh position and lead it back into ready stance. Practice 10 times with each leg. *Note:* In the beginning, practice this move very slowly. Repeat the entire sequence of moves as you concentrate on each phase. When you are more familiar with the moves, then produce them with added power.

4.0a

4.0b

4.0c

4.0d

5.0a

4.1 *Front snap kick out of forward stance (groin level):* Begin in left forward stance. With fists at waist, lift right thigh to the front and perform front snap kick. Now, put right leg down into right forward stance and raise left leg to perform front snap kick. Practice 10 times each leg, moving five times straight ahead, turning, and moving five times ahead in the opposite direction. Turn again and repeat.

5.0 *Forefist punch:* a. In ready stance, rest your right fist at hip with palm facing up. Stretch out left fist with palm facing down. *b.* and *c.* Now, pull back left fist to hip and deliver punch at solar plexus (upper stomach area) with right fist. It is important that fists nearly touch each other as they lead forward and back. Also, turn both fists just before striking final position. Practice left forefist punch 10 times, then right forefist punch 10 times. *Note:* Do not twist upper body while performing forefist punches.

5.0b

5.0c

5.1 *Forefist punch in forward stance:* *a.* Fall into left forward stance with left fist in front, right fist at hip. *b.* Lead right foot next to left and step forward into right forward stance. Shortly before reaching final stance position, perform right forefist punch and continue sequence of moves on alternate side. Practice 10 times each side; turn after five.

PERFORM RELAX STRETCH. See page 39 for instructions.

6.0 *Face punch:* Take ready stance. Extend left fist to chin level and rest right fist at hip. Now punch with right fist at chin level, pulling left fist back to hip. *Note:* The only difference between the face punch and the forefist punch is the height of your target.

6.1 *Face punch in forward stance:* Same moves as forefist punch in forward stance (5.1) except that these punches are delivered at chin level (*a.* and *b.*).

E. STRETCHES

7.0 *Ritual cool-down stretch:* See page 39 for instructions.

F. MEDITATION

5.1a

5.1b

6.1a

6.1b

PROGRAM 2

The martial arts are defensive in nature. Although certain moves can be used offensively, the discipline was developed as a form of self-defense for people whose superiors forbade them the use of weapons.

Program 2 introduces a very valuable reflex that we all have: the block. An opponent attempts a punch, and you automatically block it. That's good. What is not so good is that you also, just as automatically, step back or away. Tae kwon do teaches you to block and then, taking the initiative, move in closer to deliver a kick or a blow to your opponent.

Practice through repetition is the most important teaching tool we have. By repeating some of the moves given in Program 2, you will reinforce a natural reflex: to block a blow. By repeating other moves, also given here, you will learn to substitute a defensive technique, such as the front snap kick, for that of turning away or stepping back.

The techniques introduced in Program 2 are very basic. For those of you interested in tae kwon do as a self-defense discipline, you will quickly learn that basic is best. A few years ago, the two of us were involved in a street fight that had us outnumbered two to one. Neither of us were terribly proficient in the art of tae kwon do at the time, but we did know how to deliver a good front snap kick and a forefist punch. If it had been possible to run away, we would have. But faced with a small gang, we could only react as we had been taught. The basics may have saved our lives.

A. MEDITATION

B. STRETCHES

1.0 *Warm-up stretch.* See pages 26–36 for instructions.

C. ABDOMINALS

See pages 43–45 for instructions.

D. REPEAT TECHNIQUES

2.0 *Front snap kick in ready stance:* Introduced in Program 1, this move should be repeated 15 times on each leg.

3.0 *Forefist punch in ready stance:* Introduced in Program 1. Repeat 20 times on each arm.

4.0 *Face punch in ready stance:* Introduced in Program 1. Repeat 20 times on each arm.

E. NEW TECHNIQUES

5.0 *Front snap kick/forefist punch combination in forward stance:* Begin in left forward stance. Keep left fist stretched out in front, your right fist held at hip. Lift right thigh and snap kick. As you fall into the right forward stance, perform right forefist punch. Practice each side 10 times; turn after five times.

6.0 *Low block:* This is our first defensive move. It is used to block an attack at abdomen and groin level.

6.1 *Low block in ready stance:* Strike the ready stance, hands in fists. *a.* Raise left arm so that palm faces right ear. Lower right arm with palm of hand covering groin. *b.* Lower left arm toward left knee, as you pull back right arm to right hip. *c.* At the last moment, turn fists 180 degrees so that your left arm covers groin and knee areas and your right fist is at hip, ready for possible counterattack. In this particular move, the blocking area is the forearm. *Important:* The left arm must be brought down as hard and as fast as the right arm, which is drawn back for a possible attack punch. Repeat this maneuver 20 times on each side. Perform the first few repetitions slowly. Later, when you've memorized the moves, increase the velocity.

6.1a

6.1b

6.1c

6.2 *Low block in forward stance: a.* Begin in left forward stance. As with the technique just performed, your left arm is lowered over groin/knee area, your right fist is positioned at right hip. *b.* Now, as you fall into right forward stance, lead right fist to left ear and cover groin with left fist. *c.* Perform right low block shortly before reaching final stance position. Practice each side 10 times; turn after five times.

6.2a

6.2b

6.2c

7.1a

7.1b

7.0 *High block:* The high block is applied to protect your upper body from any attacks.

7.1 *High block in ready stance: a.* Cross arms in front of your chest at a three-fist distance, palms facing chest. When performing a right high block, the blocking arm (right) is crossed in front of your punching arm (left). *b.* From this position, quickly raise your right arm to your head with approximately a three-fist distance between fist and forehead. As you raise your right arm, bring your left arm down to the left hip. Before striking the final position, twist both wrists at the very last moment. To perform a left high block, cross arms in front of you. Since your left arm is now the blocking arm, it is crossed in front of the right, which, in this case,

functions as your punching arm. Perform 20 times each side.

7.2 *High block in forward stance:* Strike left forward stance as you perform a left high block. Move forward into right forward stance. As you take this stance, perform the right high block so hand and feet moves coincide. While you step forward, cross arms in front of chest. Ten times each side.

8.0 *Back stance:* The back stance is very convenient. From this position you can easily move into any other stance by simply stepping forward or backward. In the left back stance, your right foot is positioned 24 inches directly behind the left and is turned out at a 90-degree angle. Seventy percent of your weight is on the rear (right) foot and 30 percent is on your front (left) foot. The weight is distributed in these percentages so you can easily lift your front leg for a counterattack. In the final stance position, both knees are turned out.

8.1 *Back stance at wall:* To ensure a proper stance, practice the back stance against a wall. Lean with your back flat to the wall, your left foot straight in front of you, your right foot turned out at a 90-degree angle to the right. Turn head to the left and lift your arms, hands in fists.

8.0

8.2a

8.2 *Moving in back stance: a.* Strike the right back stance. Lift your hands into fists. Right fist is held in front of you with your left one positioned at chest level. *b.* and *c.* Now, shift weight onto right leg and bring rear (left) foot forward along with your left fist as you pull back right fist. Ten times on each side.

8.2b

8.2c

9.0 *High front snap kick in ready stance:* Begin in ready stance. Raise your right thigh as high as possible. Snap foreleg forward as you push your hip forward. Your foot must be flexed. Keep your thigh extended, but pull back your calf so that leg forms a 90-degree angle. Bring leg to start position. While performing the high front snap kick, your hands are in fists and held high to protect your face. Practice 20 times with each leg. Execute the moves slowly at first, then gradually build power in your later repetitions. *Note:* The higher you raise your knee in preparatory phase, the higher you will be able to kick.

9.1 *High front snap kick in forward stance:* Fall into the left forward stance, your hands in fists and held in front of hips. Now, put right foot next to left, raise your right thigh, and execute a right high front snap kick. Let your right leg fall into a right forward stance. If you cannot kick at chin level, then kick at chest level—or as high as you are able to kick. Ten times on each side.

9.2 *High front snap kick in back stance:* Begin in left back stance. Raise right thigh as high as possible in the front and perform a right high front snap kick. Lead your leg into right back stance. Perform 10 times on each side.

9.0

10.0a

10.0b

10.0c

F. COMBINATION

10.0 *High front snap kick out of forward stance with high block: a.* Strike a left forward stance and *b.* execute a right high front snap kick. *c.* Drop leg into a right forward stance as you perform a right high block; these two moves are executed simultaneously.

G. STRETCHES

11.0 *Ritual cool-down stretch:* See page 39 for instructions. Do not ignore these stretches. In building up strength and endurance, your muscles can also become tight and lose their elasticity. These stretches will relax your body and keep it extended.

H. MEDITATION

PROGRAM 3

As your command of tae kwon do grows, you should concentrate on those moves which will add power to your technique. The roundhouse kick is one such move. As opposed to the front snap kick, which is delivered straight on, the roundhouse kick comes from the side. While this might seem to make it a weaker kick, the opposite is true. To demonstrate, try throwing a ball without taking your hand behind your shoulder. Now try it again, but let your hand go as far back as possible. Which throw has more power?

Because it takes longer to execute, the roundhouse kick is not as practical in a street situation as the front snap kick. It is, however, much more powerful.

In Program 3, we introduce the roundhouse kick with the horse stance; it is a stance that develops your legs and gives them stamina. The horse stance is low, and after practicing it only a very short time, you will feel a burning in your thighs. In the beginning, it's not a very pleasant sensation, but it means you are building strength—strength you'll need to execute all kicks, especially the powerful roundhouse kick.

A. MEDITATION

B. STRETCHES

1.0 *Warm-up stretch:* See pages 26–36 for instructions.

C. ABDOMINALS

See pages 43–45 for instructions.

D. REPEAT TECHNIQUES

2.0 *Low block in ready stance:* Introduced in Program 2. Perform 10 times on each side.

5.0

3.0 *High block in ready stance:* Introduced in Program 2. Perform 10 times on each side.

4.0 *High front snap in ready stance:* Introduced in Program 2. Perform 10 times on each side.

PERFORM RELAX STRETCH.

E. NEW TECHNIQUES

5.0 *Horse stance:* Feet straight ahead, position them double shoulder width apart with your knees turned out. Hold fists at head level. Abdominals must be held tightly. Fall out of ready stance and into horse stance; perform 10 times.

5.1

5.1 *Forefist punch solar plexus in horse stance:* Begin horse stance. Stretch out left fist while holding right fist at hip. From this position, deliver alternating right and left forefist punches solar plexus high. Practice 20 times on each side. *Important:* The arm which descends to hip must be pulled back with the same velocity as your punch.

5.2 *Face punch in horse stance:* Strike horse stance. Hold left fist out in front, right fist at hip. Now, deliver a right face punch at chin level. Practice 20 times on each side. *Relax:* Shake arms and legs for 15 seconds.

5.3 *Double forefist punch (doublet) in horse stance at solar plexus:* Begin in horse stance. Left fist is held out, right fist is at hip. *This time* punch with right fist, then follow immediately with a left fist punch. (One punch follows the other with rapid-fire motion in a right/left punch sequence so that you end up in starting position.) Perform 10 times in right/left punch sequence. *Then* repeat 10 times in a left/right punch sequence.

5.4a

5.4b

5.4 *Moving in horse stance:* a. Begin in horse stance. With head turned to the right, hold fists at head level. *b.* Now, put your left foot behind your right, and then move your right foot to the right, placing the feet a double shoulder width apart. (*Important:* Do not let your arms down. Keep hands in fists.) Practice 10 times on each side. When turning after five times, simply turn your head to the left and complete a horse stance turn.

6.0 *Roundhouse kick:* Unlike the front snap kick, which is executed in a straight line, the roundhouse kick follows a half-circle line. The move may not be as quick, but it does develop more power along its path to the target.

6.1 *Roundhouse kick out of forward stance (in place):* a. Begin in left forward stance. b. Raise your right knee to the outside at hip level. *c.* As you snap calf forward, simultaneously pivot left foot 180 degrees back. Kick at hip level and do not forget to push your hip forward. *d.* Now, pull back leg, *e.* leading it back into left forward stance. *Important:* Keep fists at head level to protect face. Flex right foot when kicking (instep or shin is area of impact). Practice 20 times on each side.

6.1a

6.1b

6.1c

6.1d

6.1e

6.2 *Roundhouse kick out of forward stance (moving forward):* Begin in left forward stance. With hands in fists, raise right knee up to hip level at the side, execute round-house kick, and putting down your right foot, fall into right forward stance. *Remember:* The higher you raise your knee in the preparatory phase of the round-house kick, the easier it will be for you to deliver this move properly. Practice 10 times on each side.

PERFORM RELAX STRETCH.

F. COMBINATION

7.0 *Roundhouse kick in forward stance with face punch: a.* Strike left forward stance along with a left face punch. Raise right leg to hip level to the side and *b.* execute a roundhouse kick as you turn left foot back almost 180 degrees. *c.* Perform a right face punch at the moment you bring right leg down into right forward stance. Practice 10 times on each leg. Turn after five repetitions.

G. STRETCH

8.0 *Ritual cool-down stretch:* See page 39 for instructions.

H. MEDITATION

7.0a

7.0b

PROGRAM 4

Every exercise program must begin with a routine of stretches that relax and extend the body, preparing it for the more strenuous workout to come. Many people find these stretches the most boring part of any exercise regimen, and it's not uncommon to see joggers and weight lifters who perform no stretches before they start their core workouts. Injuries and soreness are often the result of this kind of shortcutting. In tae kwon do, the stretch regimen will help prevent pulled ligaments and muscles, but it is also necessary for another equally important reason: Stretches are the only way to develop the kind of flexibility needed to perform high kicks, an integral part of tae kwon do. High kicks are impossible to execute if the body is not extended, that is, "stretched out."

In actual street combat situations, the high kick is rarely used. Low kicks, which are quicker and more powerful, are preferred for obvious reasons. High kicks, however, are important to the development of a good technique. In practicing them, you gain the kind of control that will make your low kicks even more powerful. In other words, if you can do it high, you'll have no problem executing a great low kick.

A. MEDITATION

B. STRETCHES

1.0 *Warm-up stretch:* See pages 26–36 for instructions.

C. ABDOMINALS

See pages 43–45 for instructions.

D. REPEAT TECHNIQUES

2.0 *Forefist punch in horse stance:* Introduced in Program 3. Perform 20 times on each side.

3.0 *Face punch in horse stance:* Introduced in Program 3. Perform 20 times on each side.

4.0 *Doublet in horse stance:* Introduced in Program 3. Perform 20 times on each side.

5.0 *Front snap kick in forward stance (in place):* Introduced in Program 2. Perform 20 times on each leg.

PERFORM RELAX STRETCH.

E. NEW TECHNIQUES

6.0 *High roundhouse kick:* This move travels in a circle as opposed to a straight line like the snap kick. The kicking foot must be flexed, and like all other kicks, it is delivered with a snap. The only difference between this kick and the roundhouse kick is the height of your target. The high roundhouse kick is aimed at chin level.

6.1 *High roundhouse kick in forward stance (in place):* Begin in left forward stance, raise right knee as high as possible in a circle that travels from the side of your body to the front. Thigh and calf are held at a 45-degree angle to each other (knee-calf position). Shortly before leg reaches front position, kick and turn left foot 180 degrees back. Pull back the calf of your kicking leg as fast as possible so that your thigh and calf are once again at a 45-degree angle to each other, then back into left forward stance. *Important:* During the snapping phase of the kick, your hips must also be pushed forward to achieve the proper "shock" effect. Beginners may find it difficult to kick at chin level. Do not overestimate your abilities. In the beginning, a high roundhouse kick at chest level, or even a bit higher than groin level, can be looked upon as a success. Perform 10 times each leg.

6.2 *Moving high roundhouse kick in forward stance:* With hands held in fists, strike a left forward stance. Raise right leg into pulled knee-

6.0

calf position and kick. Bring leg down into right forward stance. Perform 10 times each leg.

7.0 *Middle inside block:* This block is best used against attacks directed to your hips, ribs, or chest.

7.1 *Middle inside block in forward stance (in place): a.* The block begins with your left fist tucked underneath your right armpit. The palm of your fist almost touches your right inner upper arm. The palm of your right fist lies one-fist distance above the left outer upper arm. *b.* Keeping your arm bent, lead left arm outward at shoulder level as you turn arm over. Arm stops in center of chest. *c.* While the left arm is led outward, your right travels along hip for a possible counterattack. A shock effect is achieved by twisting both fists prior to striking final position. Tense your abdominals at the very last moment. Perform 20 times. Move into right forward stance and perform middle inside block with right arm 20 times.

7.2 *Moving middle inside block in forward stance:* Perform 10 times on each side. (Turn after five times.)

7.1a

7.1b

7.1c

F. COMBINATION

8.0 *Middle inside block in forward stance with high front snap kick:* Begin in ready stance. *a.* As you fall into right forward stance, lead the right blocking arm under left armpit. This is the preparatory phase for the middle inside block. *b.* Before reaching final stance position, execute a right middle inside block. *c.* Now deliver a left high front snap kick, keeping your right fist up and your left fist at hip. Quickly pull leg back into a right forward stance. Next, move into left forward stance and deliver simultaneously a left middle inside block. Now execute a right high front snap kick. Finally, pull back right leg and fall back into a left forward stance.

G. STRETCHES

9.0 *Ritual cool-down stretch:* See page 39 for instructions.

H. MEDITATION

8.0a

8.0b

8.0c

PROGRAM 5

While the martial arts can be an effective exercise regimen, their foundation as a form of self-defense must not be overlooked. In Program 5, we focus on this fundamental aspect of the discipline. Tae kwon do is not taught as a means to inflict harm. It is not an offensive program. But face to face with an aggressor, tae kwon do experts know how to protect themselves, and this entails knowing where their opponents are the most vulnerable.

Side kicks are very effective in self-defense because the knee area—the obvious target—is one of the weakest points on the body. As you have already learned, certain moves are performed repeatedly in classroom or practice situations so that you can, in time, recall them without making a conscious effort of it. You do not think, you simply do. The side kick, introduced in Program 5, is such a move. If delivered in a combat situation, it is a means of self-defense that the martial arts expert can recall automatically and without effort, saving all mental and physical faculties to focus on his or her goal.

A. MEDITATION

B. STRETCHES

1.0 *Warm-up stretch:* See pages 26–36 for instructions.

C. ABDOMINALS

See pages 43–45 for instructions.

D. REPEAT MOVES

2.0 *Low block in ready stance:* Introduced in Program 2. Practice 10 times each side.

3.0 *High block in ready stance:* Introduced in Program 2. Practice 10 times each side.

4.0 *Middle inside block in ready stance:* Introduced in Program 4. Practice 10 times each side.

5.0 *Front snap kick in ready stance:* Introduced in Program 2. Practice 10 times each side.

6.0 *High roundhouse kick in ready stance:* Introduced in Program 4. Practice 10 times each side.

PERFORM RELAX STRETCH.

E. NEW MOVES

7.0 *Low block with forefist punch in ready stance:* Begin in ready stance. *a.* Palm of left fist faces right ear. Right fist protects groin area with your arm completely extended. *b.* and *c.* Left arm is led downward to groin. Right fist is pulled back to hip. *d.* Now execute a right forefist punch as you simultaneously pull left fist back to hip. Perform 10 times on each side.

PERFORM   CONDITIONING AND RELAX STRETCHES.

7.0a

7.0b

7.0c

7.0d

8.0 *Middle side kick:* As the name suggests, the side kicks are executed to the side of your body. They can, however, be applied in any direction and at a target of any height. Beginners should start with low targets in order to learn the proper performance of this technique. A side kick delivered at groin level is called the middle side kick. The low side kick is performed at knee level. This low leg kick is easy to do, but is very effective in self-defense as the knee is one of the weakest areas of the body. The high side kick, directed at the chest and head, requires great flexibility, making it very difficult for the beginner to perform.

To execute a middle side kick, *a.* bring your right foot to the inside of your left knee. The kicking foot is turned in to your body and foot points down to the floor, toes flexed. *b.* Now, kick the foot in a straight line to the side at hip level while your left foot turns 90 degrees to your left. For added power, push hip into kicking movement. Imagine hitting your target with the edge of your foot, toes flexed. *Important:* To support your kick, make a right sidefist punch at the same time that you kick. (A sidefist punch is like a forefist punch, with two differences: it is executed to the side instead of to the front, and your palm faces forward instead of down.) Hold left fist at hip for a possible counterattack. *c.* After completing the kick, bring your leg back to inside of left knee as fast as possible, ensuring great power.

8.0

8.0b

8.3a

8.3b

8.1 *Middle side kick with hold at wall (or chair):* To learn the correct kicking movement, lean against a wall (or chair) with one hand, the right shoulder facing the wall. Now, raise left knee so that left foot almost touches right knee joint and perform middle side kick with left leg. Let leg stay in air for a moment before you lead leg back into inner knee joint position. Ten times each side.

8.2 *Middle side kick in horse stance (in place):* Begin in horse stance. Raise right leg to inside of left knee and kick to the side. Lead leg back to knee, then fall back into horse stance. Perform 10 times on each side.

8.3 *Middle side kick in horse stance (moving):* a. Fall into horse stance, hands in fists. b. Looking to the right, cross left foot behind right foot and raise right leg to inside of left knee. Now, c. perform middle side kick to right side, supporting kick with a right sidefist punch. Then, pull right leg back into inside of the left knee and step to the side with right foot, striking a new horse stance position. Perform 10 times on each leg. Turn after five times just by looking to your left.

PERFORM RELAX STRETCH.

9.0 *Low side kick:* This kick is very effective in real combat situations. It is performed like a middle side kick but at a lower level. With toes flexed, bring your left foot to inside of right knee. From this position, kick your left leg out in a straight line at knee level and pull back with equal velocity. As with the middle kick, support this kick with a left sidefist punch and turn your right foot 90 degrees back.

9.1 *Low side kick in ready stance (in place):* Strike ready stance, looking left. Execute low side kick. Perform 10 times on each side, alternating right and left side.

F. STRETCHES

10.0 *Ritual cool-down stretches:* See page 39 for instructions.

G. MEDITATION

8.3c

PROGRAM 6

The martial arts are based upon a philosophy of action in which the mind and the body operate as one. You have already learned that this oneness of self allows you to react without thinking. It is a state of being that you must achieve if you are to spar effectively despite the body's limitations.

You are exhausted. Your body has been weakened after an extended match with an opponent. You can only continue a minute or two longer. While your body is almost ready to quit, it is your mind that gives you the direction to continue. Here's how your mind and your body can be taught to operate as one:

As always, your eyes must remain focused. Even though your limbs are ready to collapse, you keep your concentration. You do not think about the future and what might happen to your already exhausted limbs 60 seconds from now. Only the present exists. Relying upon the reflexes that you have acquired through long hours of practice, you execute a surprise move, such as the back kick. Taken off guard, your opponent will momentarily lose his focus. His concentration will be broken. Even his balance may be upset, and you, reacting quickly to his confusion, suddenly find yourself at an advantage.

When you are exhausted, you can't go on forever. For this reason, you must create a situation that will quickly put you at an advantage. Generally, this can only be achieved by injecting an element of surprise into your sparring technique. The back kick, introduced in Program 6, will do just that.

A. MEDITATION

B. STRETCHES

1.0 *Warm-up stretch:* See pages 26–36 for instructions.

C. ABDOMINALS

See pages 43–45 for instructions.

D. REPEAT MOVES

2.0 *Front snap kick in ready stance:* Introduced in Program 2. Practice 10 times on each leg.

3.0 *Roundhouse kick in ready stance:* Introduced in Program 3. Practice 10 times on each side.

4.0 *Middle side kick in ready stance:* Introduced in Program 5. Practice 10 times on each side.

5.0 *Low side kick in ready stance:* Introduced in Program 5. Practice 10 times on each leg.

PERFORM RELAX STRETCH.

E. NEW MOVES

6.0 *Moving low side kick in horse stance:* Looking to the right, strike horse stance with fists at head level. Put left foot behind right, raising right foot to inside of left knee. Perform low side kick, which is supported by right sidefist punch; at the same time, left

foot is turned 90 degrees back for added balance. Now, step forward into new horse stance. *Important:* When you kick, snap the leg and pull it back with equal velocity in order to achieve a shock effect and optimum power. Perform 10 times each leg.

PERFORM RELAX STRETCH.

7.0 *Back kick:* This kick is very effective because it uses the element of surprise in its execution. As the name implies, you turn your back to the opponent and kick out like a horse.

7.1 *Back kick from wall or chair:* Like the middle side kick, the

7.2a

7.2b

back kick is best exercised, or practiced, when you have the firm support of a chair or wall. With both hands, lean against a wall or chair, raise knee to chest, foot almost touching buttocks (heel-buttocks position). Now kick back. This kick has to travel along a straight line from front to back. To have adequate shock effect,

the leg must be kicked and pulled back to the buttocks with equal velocity. During all phases of the kick, keep eye contact with your imaginary target. Perform 10 times each side.

7.2 *Moving back kick in back stance:* *a.* Strike left back stance, hands held in fists. *b.* Turn body 90 degrees to your right by turning left foot back about 180 degrees to the right, right foot back about 90 degrees, and moving right foot slightly over to the right. Knees slightly bent. *c.* Now, raise right leg into heel-buttocks position, and *d.* execute a right back kick. Pull leg back into heel-buttocks position, then step forward into right back stance. *Important:* The faster you turn your body, the easier this move will be to execute. Always move on the balls of your feet. Keep upper body slightly bent for balance. A slight swing of your arms when you pivot will also help your balance.

F. COMBINATION

8.0 *Middle side kick in horse stance with a back kick:* Looking to the right, fall into a horse stance. Fists are held in front of your body at head level. Now place left foot behind right foot, letting only the ball of your left foot touch the floor. Then bring right foot to inside of left knee and perform a middle side kick. Let right leg fall into horse stance. From this position, raise left leg into heel-buttocks position and perform back kick. Let left leg fall into horse stance as your head turns to the left. Perform 10 times on each leg.

G. STRETCHES

9.0 *Ritual cool-down stretch:* See page 39 for instructions.

H. MEDITATION

7.2c

7.2d

PROGRAM 7

It's time to put it all together. Program 7 puts the emphasis on sparring combinations. In a fight situation, a block is of little use unless you know what to follow it with: a kick? a stance? Or perhaps a punch? No one particular technique is always correct.

Program 7 introduces a number of prearranged sparring combinations, as we call them, that can be used in a match. By repeating these combinations over and over again in a practice situation, you will, in time, be able to recall them without having to make a conscious effort of it.

The word "combination" is also used in ballet. A turn followed by a jump followed by some fancy step work is a set of moves that is, in performance, a prearranged combination. The same is true in the martial arts. The difference here is that your opponent provides a variable that does not exist in dance. Because an opponent can use many different moves against you, you need to memorize a variety of prearranged sparring combinations. Regardless of what your opponent does, you must be able to respond automatically.

A. MEDITATION

B. STRETCHES

1.0 *Warm-up stretch:* See pages 26–36 for instructions.

C. ABDOMINALS

See pages 43–45 for instructions.

D. REPEAT MOVES

2.0 *High block in ready stance:* Introduced in Program 2. Perform 10 times on each side.

3.0 *Low block in ready stance:* Introduced in Program 2. Perform 10 times on each side.

4.0 *Middle outside block in ready stance:* Introduced in Program 4. Perform 10 times on each side.

5.0 *Middle side kick in ready stance:* Introduced in Program 5. Perform 10 times on each side.

E. REPEAT COMBINATIONS

6.0 *High block with forefist punch in ready stance:* Introduced in Program 5. Perform 10 times on each side.

7.0 *Low block with forefist punch in ready stance:* Introduced in Program 5. Perform 10 times on each side.

PERFORM RELAX STRETCH.

F. NEW COMBINATIONS

8.0 *Moving low block with forefist punch and roundhouse kick in forward stance: a.* Out of ready stance, *b.* step into left forward stance. As you are about to reach final stance position, perform left low block. *c.* Now, execute a right forefist punch in place, *d.* followed by a right roundhouse kick. *e.* Let leg drop into right forward stance. Shortly before reaching final position, perform a right low block followed by a left forefist punch. Repeat combination. Perform 10 times on each side.

9.0 *Moving high block with forefist punch and back kick in back stance:* Out of ready stance, step into left back stance. As you are about to reach the final position of this stance, perform a left high block. Now execute a right forefist punch in place, followed by a right back kick. Hands held in fists, let right leg fall down into right back stance. Shortly before reaching final position, execute right high block and left forefist punch followed by left back kick. *Note:* When executing the right forefist punch, pull the fist back into starting position after delivering the punch. This drawback motion will help in twisting your

8.0a

8.0b

8.0c

8.0d

8.0e

11.0a

11.0b

body as you go into the back kick. Perform 10 times on each side.

PERFORM RELAX STRETCH.

10. *Middle inside block with forefist punch in ready stance:* Begin in ready stance. Perform right middle inside block with your right arm. Now deliver a left forefist punch. *Important:* Always tense abdominals just before the block

and punch are delivered. Perform 10 times on each side.

11.0 *Moving middle inside block with middle side kick in horse stance:* Out of ready stance, move right foot forward into horse stance. *a.* and

11.0c

11.0d

b. As you are about to reach the final position of the horse stance, perform right middle inside block. *c.* Now, placing ball of left foot on the floor behind right foot, *d.* execute a right middle side kick. As you are about to put right leg down into new horse stance, perform a right middle inside block. These two moves should be performed simultaneously. Perform 10 times on each side.

PERFORM RELAX STRETCH.

G. STRETCHES

13.0 *Ritual cool-down stretch:* See page 39 for instructions.

H. MEDITATION

PROGRAM 8

Program 8 introduces a very simple technique: the knee kick. Sometimes it is necessary to isolate a part of the body to discover its strength. You won't have to perform many repetitions of the knee kick to realize the power inherent in this simple move. It requires little strength, but can be used with great effect in a sparring situation.

The knee kick is such a simple technique that you might wonder why it was not introduced in one of our earlier programs. Program 8, however, is a good point in your development at which to reflect on how well you are executing what you have already learned. Everyone executes certain techniques better than others. But why? Are you more proficient in some areas because you practice them more, or is it that those particular techniques complement your body's attributes and do not draw attention to its limitations? Certain limitations, expecially those which are the result of age, cannot be overlooked. However, it is dangerous to focus on them to the point that we wish for something that can never be. Better to emphasize your strengths and, for example, execute a superb kick to the knee if you can't hit the chest as your target.

Every body has its limitations. The important thing is to recognize yours and work out a strategy that will, in a sparring situation, emphasize what you do best.

A. MEDITATION

B. STRETCHES

1.0 *Warm-up stretch:* See pages 26–36 for instructions.

C. ABDOMINALS

See pages 43–45 for instructions.

D. REPEAT MOVES

2.0 *High block in ready stance:* Introduced in Program 2. Perform 10 times on each side.

3.0 *Low block in ready stance:* Introduced in Program 2. Perform 10 times on each side.

4.0 *Middle inside block in ready stance:* Introduced in Program 4. Perform 10 times on each side.

5.0 *Front snap kick in ready stance:* Introduced in Program 1. Perform 10 times on each side.

6.0 *Roundhouse kick in ready stance:* Introduced in Program 3. Perform 10 times on each side.

7.0 *Middle side kick in ready stance:* Introduced in Program 5. Perform 10 times on each side.

PERFORM RELAX STRETCH.

E. NEW TECHNIQUES

8.0 *Knee kick:* This technique is used only in infights, that is, combat situations that are physically very close. It is the easiest leg move to learn because you simply raise your knee. It is, however, very powerful. Hitting area is upper knee.

8.1 *Knee kick in ready stance:* Strike a ready stance, hands in fists at hips. With a pointed toe, raise your left knee as high as possible to chest. *Important:* As your knee ascends, push hips forward very slightly. This helps to ensure a shock effect. However, don't take your upper body back too far. *Note:* Even though it is called a knee *kick*, the foot and shin remain under the knee and do not shoot out, as they would in a real kick. Perform 10 times each side.

8.2 *Moving knee kick in forward stance:* With fists held at hip, strike a left forward stance. Perform a right knee kick, then put leg down into a right forward stance. Perform 10 times each side.

9.0 *Forward knee kick:* Similar to the simple knee kick, the forward

8.1

knee kick is even more powerful because it involves a greater degree of your body weight. Hitting area is right below your knee-cap.

9.1 *Forward knee kick in back stance (in place):* Begin in left back stance. Raise right knee to hip level in the front and then push hip forward. Unlike the knee kick, which requires that your back only tilt slightly, the forward knee kick must be executed with a 20-degree bend in your back. Upon completion of the kick, pull your leg back into left back stance. Perform 10 times each leg.

9.2 *Jump forward knee kick in back stance:* With fists at hip level, fall into left back stance. Jump forward as you execute a right forward knee kick. Land in right back stance. *Note:* Do not jump straight up into the air. The jump is directed forward, not up.

9.1

9.2.

F. NEW COMBINATIONS

10.0 *Moving front snap kick with knee kick in forward stance:* Begin in left forward stance and perform a right front snap kick. Put leg down into right forward stance. Now, perform knee kick with left leg and pull left knee back into right forward stance. Next, execute left front snap kick followed by right knee kick. *Note:* This is a knee kick, not a forward knee kick. It is directed in to your chest, not out. Your back tilts only slightly. Perform 10 times on each side.

PERFORM RELAX STRETCH.

11.0 *Double forefist punch with face punch in horse stance:* Begin in horse stance. *a.* Extend left arm, rest right fist on hip. *b.* Using right/left/right punch sequence, execute double forefist punch starting with a right punch to solar plexus, *c.* then a left punch to solar plexus, *d.* followed by a right face punch. Then repeat using the left/right/left punch sequence. Continue to repeat sequence. Twenty times.

12.0 *Triple forefist punch with forward knee kick in back stance:* As you step into left back stance, perform a triple forefist punch (target: solar plexus), starting with your right fist. Leave right arm extended and deliver a right forward knee kick ending in right back stance. Now, deliver triple forefist punch (start with left fist) followed by a left forward knee kick. Perform 10 times each side. *Important:* When you turn after five times, cross arms in front of your body before you pivot. After

11.0a

11.0b

11.0c

11.0d

you turn, take arms down to hip level and deliver triple forefist punch starting with right fist.

G. STRETCHES

13.0 *Ritual cool-down stretch:* See page 39 for instructions.

H. MEDITATION

PROGRAM 9

The martial arts are distinctive among exercise programs; they build expertise. Runners and weight lifters may have the thrill of running farther or lifting more weight after extensive training. But the technique that they have after their first few weeks of working out is not that much greater than what they will acquire after a few years of training.

The martial arts are different. Your expertise builds and, as you progress, you must call upon this expertise in order to perform. This is one reason why the martial arts are a mental as well as a physical activity. Students of the martial arts rarely become bored with their chosen discipline because their mental capacities are constantly being developed and challenged.

Program 9 builds your martial arts expertise. It puts the emphasis on high kicks. Even though you will rarely use them in actual combat situations, a well-executed high kick will help to build power and control for application of your low kicks. Using these high kicks in sparring combinations will increase your expertise as well as your mental involvement with the discipline. Your mind as well as your body will continue to be challenged. And boredom will always be a stranger.

A. MEDITATION

B. STRETCHES

1.0 *Warm-up stretch:* See pages 26–36 for instructions.

C. ABDOMINALS

See pages 43–45 for instructions.

D. REPEAT TECHNIQUES

2.0 *Doublet in horse stance:* Introduced in Program 3. Perform 10 times with right/left punch sequence, then left/right punch sequence.

3.0 *Double face punch in horse stance:* Introduced in Program 1. Perform 10 times on each side.

4.0 *Low block in ready stance:* Introduced in Program 2. Perform 10 times on each sie.

5.0 *High block in ready stance:* Introduced in Program 2. Perform 10 times on each side.

6.0 *Front snap kick in ready stance:* Introduced in Program 1. Perform 10 times on each side.

7.0 *Roundhouse kick in ready stance:* Introduced in Program 3. Perform 10 times on each side.

8.0 *Middle side kick in horse stance:* Introduced in Program 5. Perform 10 times on each side.

9.0 *High front snap kick in ready stance:* Introduced in Program 2. Perform 10 times on each side.

10.0 *High roundhouse kick in ready stance:* Introduced in Program 4. Perform 10 times on each side.

PERFORM RELAX STRETCH.

E. NEW TECHNIQUES

9.0 *High side kick:* Like the middle side kick, the high side kick is carried out to the side. In order to perform this technique at chin level, you must be flexible enough to avoid injury.

9.1 *High side kick from chair (in place):* Hold the chair with your left hand. Right hand is held in fist. Lead right foot into left knee joint, then raise right knee as high as possible to your chest. Now, perform high side kick, quickly pulling leg back into the knee-joint position. *Important:* Don't forget to pivot on left foot while you execute the high side kick. Also, always remember, the higher you raise your knee to your chest in the preparatory phase, the higher you will be able to kick. Perform 10 times each side.

9.2 *High side kick in ready stance:* Place left foot at the inside of your right knee. *Raise knee as high as possible to your chest.* From this point, the kick travels to the side, reaching for chin level. Support the kick with a left side fist punch. In order to achieve the shock effect, the left hip must be pushed forward as far as possible and the leg must be pulled back after complete extension into the knee-chest position. The hitting area is the edge of the foot.

9.3 *High side kick in horse stance (in place):* Fall into a horse stance with hands in fists. Now perform right high side kick. Support the kick with a right side punch. Execute these two moves simultaneously. *Note:* If you are not flexible enough to kick at chin level, deliver the kick at chest level instead. Perform 10 times each side.

9.4 *Moving high side kick in horse stance:* Fall forward into horse stance. Put left foot behind right, then bring right foot to the inside of left knee. Now, raise leg as high as possible to chest and perform a right high side kick supported by a right forefist punch. Then pull leg back into the chest and let it fall into a new horse stance. Perform 10 times each side.

PERFORM RELAX STRETCH.

9.2

F. NEW COMBINATIONS

10.0 *Moving high front snap kick with high roundhouse kick in forward stance:* With fists at hip level, strike a left forward stance. Perform right high front snap kick, pulling the leg down into a left forward stance. Now perform right high roundhouse kick, letting your leg fall into a right forward stance. Repeat the combination, starting it this time with a left high front snap kick. Perform 10 times each side.

PERFORM RELAX STRETCH.

11.0 *Moving high roundhouse kick in forward stance and high side kick in horse stance:* Hands in fists, strike a left forward stance. Perform right high roundhouse kick, putting right leg down in front of you in a right horse stance, as you look to your right. Now place left foot behind right and perform a right high side kick. Leg falls into a right forward stance. Repeat combination, this time beginning with a left high roundhouse kick. Perform 10 times on each side.

PERFORM RELAX STRETCH.

G. STRETCHES

12.0 *Ritual cool-down stretch:* See page 39 for instructions.

H. MEDITATION

PROGRAM 10

A new stance, the fighting stance, is introduced in Program 10. You will be able to apply it to the techniques you've already learned in order to develop new combinations. These new combinations will be the basis for some fighting strategies used in the self-defense program (pages 109–121).

A. MEDITATION

B. STRETCHES

1.0 *Warm-up stretch:* See pages 26–36 for instructions.

C. ABDOMINALS

See pages 43–45 for instructions.

D. NEW TECHNIQUES

2.0 *Fighting stance:* The fighting stance is the one you should use in actual sparring situations. It has many advantages. First, the stance provides good protection against possible attacks to your legs and upper body. Second, it is a very balanced stance, and from it, all moves can be performed easily and in a very economical way.

In a left fighting stance, your feet are a little more than shoulder width apart with your legs slightly bent. Your left shoulder is slightly forward. Your left foot points straight forward while the right is at a 45-degree angle to it. In this stance, your weight rests equally on the balls of both feet.

2.0

Hold your left fist at approximately a four-fist distance in front of your face; the palm of your right fist faces the right jaw at a distance of one fist. Bend elbows inward slightly to block ribs and chest.

When moving forward or back in the fighting stance, complete one step before taking another. The foot which follows does not leave the floor. Rather, it slides into place.

2.1 *Moving in fighting stance: a.* Begin in left fighting stance. *b.* Now shift weight to right foot and slide left foot even farther forward. *c.* Then shift weight to left leg and slide right foot back into original left fighting stance position. You can also move back by first sliding your rear foot back and then your front foot. Move 10 times forward and 10 times back.

In right fighting stance your right foot is placed forward. This time your left shoulder is slightly pulled back. Move 10 times forward and 10 times back. *Important:* Don't bounce up and down. Always keep your knees bent so that your head stays on one level.

2.1a

2.1b

3.0 *Moving doublet in fighting stance:* Strike right fighting stance. As you step forward into new fighting stance, deliver a double forefist punch starting with right forefist. (These two moves are performed simultaneously.) *Important: a.* In a right forefist punch, your right shoulder moves forward in support of the punch. *b.* The left forefist punch is supported by twisting the left shoulder and left hip forward when you deliver the blow. After each punch, pull arms back into starting position. Practice five times moving forward and five times back with right/left punch. Then practice five times forward and five times back with left/right punch sequence in left fighting stance. *Note:* When performing a double forefist punch in the fighting stance, you achieve optimum power by putting your whole body into the punch.

3.1 *Jump forward knee kick in fighting stance:* Strike left fighting stance and stretch both arms out in front of you at head level (as if you were grasping somebody by the head or shoulders). Now pull your arms to your body (imagine you are pulling an opponent toward you), and at the same time perform a right forward knee kick by jumping forward at the imaginary target. Practice 10 times each side.

3.0a

3.0b

E. NEW COMBINATIONS

4.0 *Moving doublet with front snap kick in fighting stance:* Strike left fighting stance. Execute a doublet in place, then perform a right front snap kick with your arms held in fighting position. Fall into a right fighting stance as you deliver a new doublet, starting with the right fist. *Important:* Keep knees slightly bent at all times. Move on balls of feet. Perform 10 times each side. Turn after five repetitions.

PERFORM RELAX STRETCH.

5.0 *Moving doublet with front snap kick and back kick in fighting stance:* Begin in left fighting stance. Execute doublet in place, then perform right front snap kick, your arms held in fighting position. After kicking, put right leg down into right fighting stance. Now deliver a left back kick letting left leg fall into left fighting stance. Perform 10 times each leg; turn after five.

6.0 *Moving doublet with front snap kick and roundhouse kick in fighting stance:* Strike left fighting stance. Execute doublet in place, then perform right front snap kick followed by a left roundhouse kick, which falls into a left fighting stance. Perform 10 times each side; turn after five times.

PERFORM RELAX STRETCH.

10.0a

10.0b

7.0 *Moving low block with forefist punch in forward stance:* Out of ready stance, step into left forward stance. While stepping forward, put left arm to right ear and right fist in front of groin and perform a left low block. Now execute a right forefist punch in place, then step into right forward stance as you execute a right low block. Then, deliver a left forefist punch and continue combination. Perform 10 times each side. Alternate and turn after five times.

8.0 *Moving high block with forefist punch in forward stance:* Out of ready stance, step into left forward stance, executing a left high block. Now perform a right forefist punch in place. Step into right forward stance and repeat combination on other side. Perform 10 times each side.

9.0 *Moving low block and high block with forefist punch in forward stance:* Out of ready stance, step into left forward stance as you perform a left low block followed by a left high block in place and deliver a right forefist punch. Step into right forward stance and repeat combination on other side. Perform 10 times each side.

PERFORM RELAX STRETCH.

10.0c

10.0d

10.0 *Moving high block and low block in forward stance with a middle inside block in back stance and forefist punch in forward stance:* Begin in ready stance, *a.* and as you step into left forward stance, perform a left high block. *b.* Now execute a left low block. *c.* Then, as you step back with left foot into left back stance, perform a left middle inside block. *d.* Perform a right forefist punch as you step forward into right forward stance, followed by a right high block and a right low block. As you slide back into right back stance, perform a right middle inside block. Finish the combination with left forefist punch while stepping into left forward stance. Perform five times each side.

PERFORM RELAX STRETCH.

F. STRETCHES

11.0 *Ritual cool-down stretch:* See page 39 for instructions.

G. MEDITATION

SELF-DEFENSE PROGRAMS

Tae kwon do is performed around the world. In the classroom, where it is usually found, tae kwon do is a ritual of sorts. It is a highly stylized kind of martial art, performed in a controlled environment where the opponents are anything but enemies. An etiquette of action is always obeyed.

In a less controlled environment, such as the street, there is little place for ritual. Etiquette does not exist. And respect for your assailant is impossible. To apply the art of tae kwon do here demands adjustments. Surprisingly, just as prearranged patterns of sparring techniques are used in the classroom, so they can be used in the street. With adjustments, of course.

Included here are eight sparring patterns which can be employed as counterattacks to many grips, punches, or kicks directed at your body. Hopefully, you will never have to use any of these self-defense patterns in a situation where your life is endangered. It is always better to run away than engage in a fight, even if you are proficient in the martial arts. The object is to survive an incident of violence, not to prove your expertise. Accept the challenge only when you have no other choice. Tae kwon do is a self-defense technique, and should never be used offensively.

The prearranged fighting patterns in this chapter can be included as part of your regular tae kwon do workout. Through repetition, these patterns will become instilled in your consciousness, making it possible for you to recall them spontaneously if you should have to use them to protect yourself.

Good self-defense, of course, involves more than knowing how to move. It also involves knowing how to act. In the martial arts, the mental is stronger than the physical. When you are on the street and face to face with the inevitable, stay as calm as possible. Try not to show fear. Always look straight into your assailant's eyes. He will telegraph his intentions a second or two before he acts. Because of your peripheral vision, you can oversee his moves and be able to act accordingly. If you were to focus on his legs, for instance, you might miss an impending punch or blow.

In street fighting, avoid fancy moves even though you may execute them effectively in the classroom. Simple moves, such as a low kick, are always more effective than difficult ones.

Do not be overly eager to show people that you are proficient in the martial arts. Some individuals are too anxious to meet the challenge.

Once you have been hit by your aggressor, concentrate on how you will defend yourself, not the wound. Keep your mind strong so that you can complete your counterattack. Never show that you have been hurt. To show injury makes your opponent feel stronger.

Following are a number of street attacks that an aggressor might use against you. Fortunately, for each attack there is a counterattack. Although strength is a definite plus in defending yourself, these counterattacks don't rely upon it. More important are quickness, body positions, and a variety of grips that act as lever—all of which can be learned and none of which is dependent upon your size or sex. Learn these counterattacks, or defense patterns, so that you can deliver them instantaneously without thought. To think is to waste valuable time, time that would be better spent delivering another kick, another punch.

1.

1. *Street situation:* An assailant, ready to inflict harm, approaches. *Your defense:* Fake face punch followed by a low side kick.

Take a stance with your feet slightly more than shoulder width apart, knees bent. Fake a face punch. At the same time, apply a low side kick to the aggressor's knee area—if possible, the knee cap. Why the kneecap? It is a very vulnerable part of the leg. If you kick against it, the knee will bend through backward.

2. *Street situation:* An assailant grabs your shoulders from the front. *Your defense:* Two-arm lever with a front snap kick and knee kick.

Take normal stance. *a.* Try to break his grip by applying a two-arm lever: Raise your arms between his arms and bring your arms down bent, your forearms hitting his arms. Upon impact, twist your arms to the outside as you push the attacker's arms away. *b.* Now deliver a front snap kick to your opponent's groin, which will cause him to bend over. *c.* When this happens, grab his neck or hair, pulling his head toward your body, and deliver a right knee kick to his head or stomach.

2.a

2.b

2.c

3.a

3. *Street situation:* An assailant grabs your neck from the front. *Your defense:* One-arm lever and back kick.

a. Attacker grabs your neck. b. Turn away from him and apply one-arm lever, raising your right arm. Upon the moment of impact, c. twist your body 180 degrees back to the left. The twisting motion will rid you of your attacker's grip. d. It also sets you up to deliver a final left back kick into his groin.

3.b

3.c

3.d

4.a

4.b

4. *Street situation:* An assailant grabs you from behind at the neck, shoulder, or chest. *Your defense:* Foot shock kick followed by a low back kick and a back kick.

a. Grab hands of attacker, then lift your leg and stamp on his foot as hard as possible. *b.* Next, a low back kick against his knee, *c.* followed by a back kick into groin.

4.c

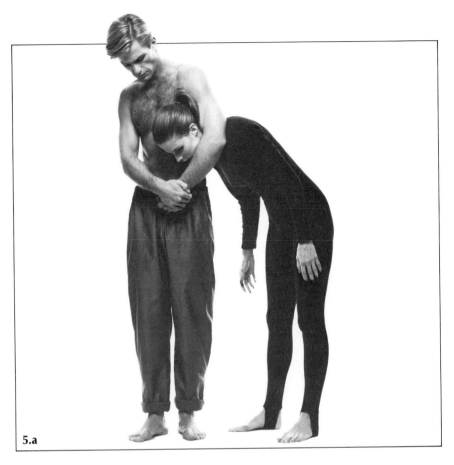

5.a

5.b

5. *Street situation:* An assailant holds you with his left arm in a suffocating grip. *Your defense:* Back/forehead lever.

a. With the assailant's arm around your neck, tense your neck muscles, bringing your chin down as hard as possible. (This move makes it almost impossible for attacker to hold his grip.) *b.* Now put your right hand on his forehead as you place left hand on his lower back. Then, push his forehead back as hard as possible as you push your left hand forward with equal pressure. The forward/backward motion is a lever technique that will break the attacker's grip.

6.a

6.b

6. *Street situation: a.* An assailant grabs your shoulder from the side with one hand. *Your defense:* Low side kick and elbow strike.

b. Fake a face punch as you deliver a low side kick to knee of assailant. *c.* Now, clasping your hands, strike his ribs or head with your elbow, putting your whole body into the blow.

6.c

7.a

7.b

7.c

7. *Street situation:* You and your assailant are face to face. *Your defense:* Sweep down block with a doublet to the face.

a. With your left arm, make a sweeping motion, pushing your assailant's arms away. *b.* and *c.* Now deliver a doublet to aggressor's face, starting with a front fist.

8. *Street situation:* An assailant makes a kick to your knee, groin, or chest area. *Your defense:* Block at knee, groin, or chest followed by a doublet.

a. Block his attack with either a low or middle inside block. *b.* and *c.* Then apply a doublet, starting with forefist at his head.

8.a

8.b

8.c

KATAS

Katas are rituals of the martial arts that have existed for centuries. Some are of more recent origin, and others, such as the three we present here, were created specially for contemporary instruction. The martial arts and their rituals continue to live!

Katas are prearranged fighting patterns that contain the techniques you have already learned. They give us a necessary repetition of fighting patterns to be used against an imaginary opponent. Katas are to be performed almost as you would a dance, each movement leading into the next without pause. If performed gracefully without interruption, katas will increase your expertise and your powers of concentration.

And concentrate you must! Katas are highly stylized. One kata will contain techniques, which you must memorize in a prearranged order. Katas always begin and end in the same stance. And even though a kata involves the performance of many moves, it concludes where it began on the floor of the classroom.

Katas are performed by every serious student of tae kwon do, or any other style of karate, for that matter. Quite often, katas are used as part of an examination to determine if a student is ready to wear a different color belt. It is through katas that we strive for perfection.

Katas can be performed as individual exercise programs or as part of a tae kwon do workout. If you perform a kata individually, be sure to meditate and complete at least 15 minutes of stretch exercises before and after you practice them.

1.

FIRST KATA
(TO FOLLOW PROGRAM 4)

1. Begin in ready stance.

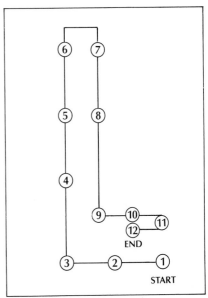

The basic pattern of the first kata is an L-shape.

2. *a.* Out of ready stance, position your left foot behind you so that it is double shoulder width apart from the right. At the same time, bring left palm to right ear and protect groin with right hand. *b.* Now turn your body 90 degrees to your left and execute a left low block as you fall into left forward stance.

3. Step forward into right forward stance and execute right forefist punch.

2.a

2.b

3

4.a

4. *a.* Place right foot next to left and bring right palm to left ear. Left fist protects groin area. *b.* Now position right foot double shoulder width apart from the left and turn body 90 degrees to your right. Execute right low block, ending in right forward stance (with feet shoulder width apart).

4.b

5.

6.

5. Step forward into left forward stance as you execute a left face punch.

6. Move forward into right forward stance as you execute a right face punch.

7.a

7.b

7.c

7. *a*. Stepping to the right with your left foot, cross arms and turn 180 degrees back. As you turn on the balls of your feet, *b*. execute a left high block and *c*. a right face punch. (Photos 7.c—9.a are shown from front.)

8.a

8.b

8. Out of left forward stance, *a.* deliver a right front snap kick, ending in right forward stance. Shortly before reaching final stance position, *b.* execute a left face punch.

9.a

9. Out of right forward stance, *a.* deliver a left roundhouse kick, *b.* falling into left forward stance as you apply left high block.

9.b

10.a

10. *a.* Turn to your right 270 degrees by placing your right foot to the left, shoulder width apart from the left foot. As you turn right, right palm moves to left ear, left fist protects groin area. *b.* Make final turn into right forward stance as you perform a right low block.

10.b

11.

12.a

12.b

11. Step forward into left forward stance and perform left forefist punch.

12. *a.* Cross fists in front of your chest. As you pivot 90° to the left, pull back your left leg and place it next to right, *b.* returning to ready stance. *Important:* Always keep your legs bent.

1.

2.a

2.b

3.a

SECOND KATA
(TO FOLLOW PROGRAM 7)

1. Begin in ready stance.

2. *a.* Slide left foot to the side and lead arms into preparatory phase for middle inside block. Pivot 90 degrees to the left and *b.* fall into left back stance. Before reaching final back stance, perform left middle inside block.

3. *a.* Perform right front snap kick, *b.* ending in right forward stance.

3.b

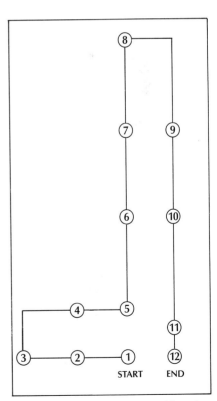

The basic pattern of the second kata is a reverse L-shape.

4.a

4.b

5.a

4. Turn 180 degrees back into right back stance as you perform right middle inside block. (This turn is accomplished by bringing right foot next to left. *a.* Now pull right foot back and cross it over to your left side, positioning your feet shoulder width apart. *b.* Turn on balls of feet and execute the block.)

5. *a.* Deliver a left front snap kick, *b.* landing in left forward stance. Hands in fists.

5.b

6. Turn 90 degrees to the left into left forward stance, performing a left low block.

7. *a.* Perform a right roundhouse kick. *b.* Put right foot down as you fall into horse stance and look to the right. Hands in fists.

8.a

8.b

8.c

8. *a.* Put left foot behind right and *b.* perform right middle side kick, *c.* ending in right back stance.

9.

10.a

10.b

9. Look over your right shoulder and perform right back kick. Turn 180 degrees and fall into right forward stance.

10. *a.* Perform a left roundhouse kick. *b.* Put left foot in front of you as you fall into horse stance, looking to left.

11.a

11.b

12.

11. Put right foot behind left and
a. deliver a left middle side kick,
b. ending in left forward stance.

12. End in ready stance by turning 180 degrees to your right.

THIRD KATA
(TO FOLLOW PROGRAM 10)

1. Begin in ready stance.

2. *a.* Turn 90 degrees to your left and fall into left forward stance. Before reaching final stance position, perform left high block and *b.* right forefist punch in place.

3. *a.* Pivot 180 degrees backward into right forward stance. Before reaching final stance position,

3.a

3.b

4.

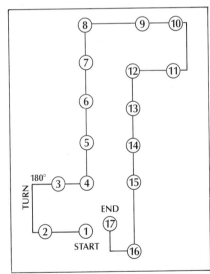

The basic pattern of the third kata is a modified Z-shape.

perform right high block and *b.* left forefist punch in place.

4. Step into left forward stance and perform right forefist punch.

5.

5. Pivot 90 degrees to the left and fall into left forward stance, performing a left low block.

6. *a.* Execute right high roundhouse kick, *b.* falling into right back stance. (Right foot in front.) Fists held at head level.

7. *a.* Turn to your left (looking over your left shoulder) and execute a left back kick, *b.* landing in left forward stance. Hands in fists.

6.a

6.b

7.a

7.b

8.a

8.b

9.a

8. *a.* Perform right front snap kick, *b.* landing in right forward stance. Hands in fists.

9. Turn 270 degrees to the left by shifting weight to the right foot, ending in left forward stance. *a.* Perform left low block, *b.* followed by a left middle inside block.

9.b

10.

10. Step forward into right forward stance as you perform a right forefist punch.

11. Turn back 180 degrees into right forward stance as you perform right low block (pictured) followed by a right high block.

12. Step into left forward stance and execute a left forefist punch.

11.

12.

13.

14.

13. Turn 90 degrees to your left and perform left low block in left forward stance.

14. Out of left forward stance, lead right foot next to your left and take one step forward with right foot, turning upper body 90 degrees to your left as you fall into right horse stance. Look to your right and perform a right middle inside block.

15.a

15.b

15. Place left foot behind right foot and *a.* perform right high side kick, *b.* landing in right horse stance. Look to right.

16.a

16. Out of right horse stance, *a.* turn 270 degrees to your left and perform a left back kick, *b.* landing in left forward stance. Hands in fists.

16.b

17. Turn 180 degrees to your right and fall into ready stance.

As you read this sentence, you probably have a different attitude towards your body than when you first began performing tae kwon do. Hopefully, you also have a very different body. Continue to perform the tae kwon do programs and you will continue to see further improvement and change. As you practice the exercises in this book, be sure not to skip over those techniques which are most difficult to perform. Those techniques are the ones which give your body's problem areas their best workout.

It is our hope that you will want to pursue the discipline of tae kwon do in the classroom. Books may end, but the study of the martial arts never does.

17.